Name _____

Identifying triangles (twenty-seven) 27

28 (twenty-eight) Practice

Name _____

Patterns: 1 shape, 2 colors **(twenty-nine)** 29

30 (thirty) Patterns: 2 shapes, 2 colors

Name _____

Activity: Coloring the same kind of shape **(thirty-one)** 31

Chapter 3

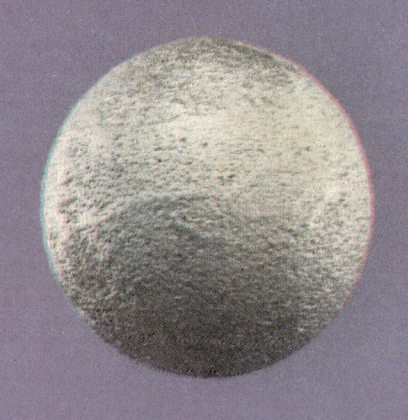

Problem Formulation: Asking questions about a situation (thirty-three) 33

34 (thirty-four) Comparing size; larger

Name

Comparing size; smaller **(thirty-five)** 35

36 (thirty-six) Patterns: 1 object, 2 colors

Name _____

Comparing size; largest (thirty-seven) 37

38 (thirty-eight) Comparing size; smallest

Name _____

Comparing size; taller **(thirty-nine)** 39

40 (forty) Comparing size; tallest

Name _____

Comparing size; longer (forty-one) 41

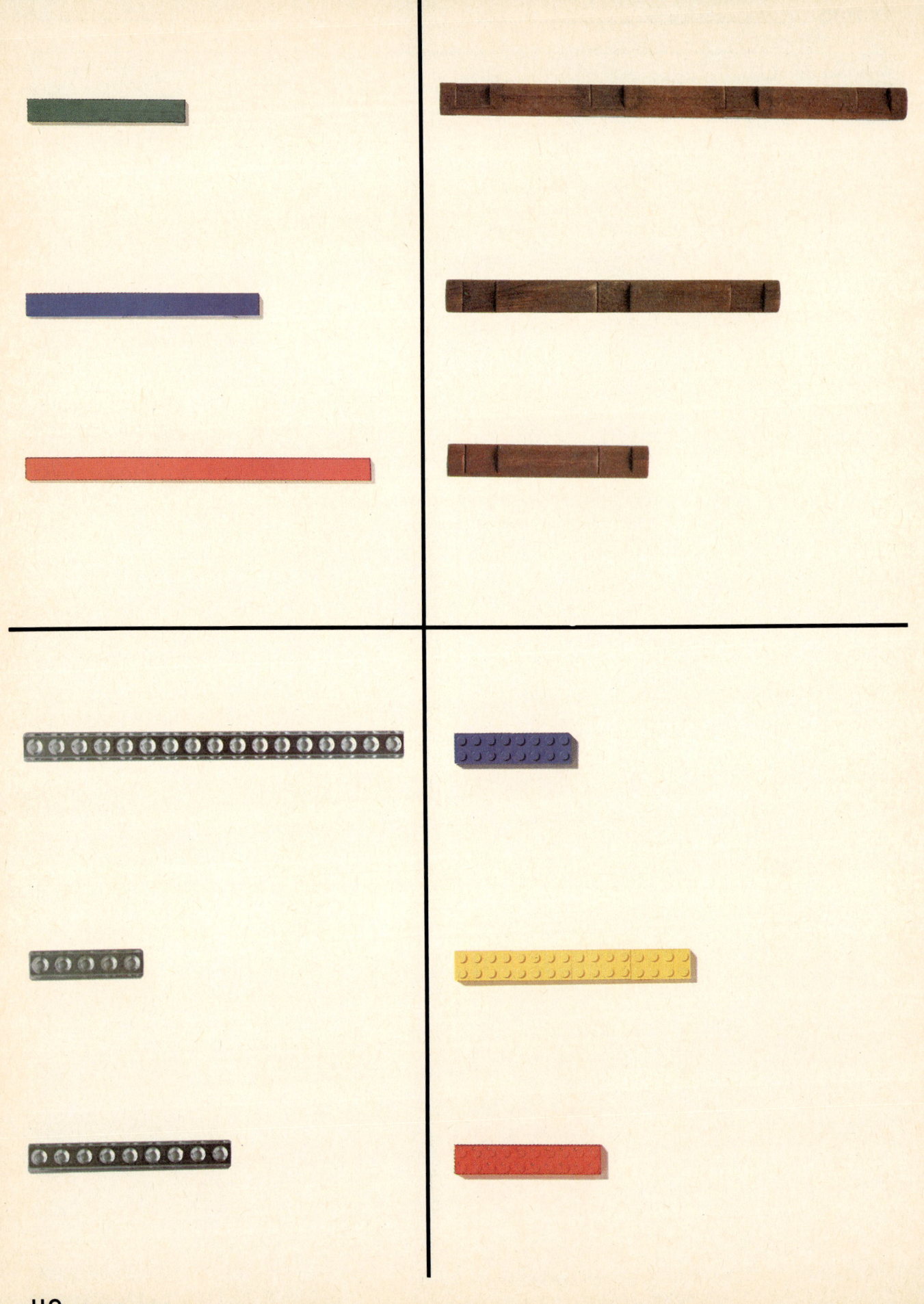

42 (forty-two) Comparing size; longest

Name _____

Recognizing more **(forty-three)** 43

44 **(forty-four)** Recognizing most

Name _____

Recognizing fewer (forty-five) 45

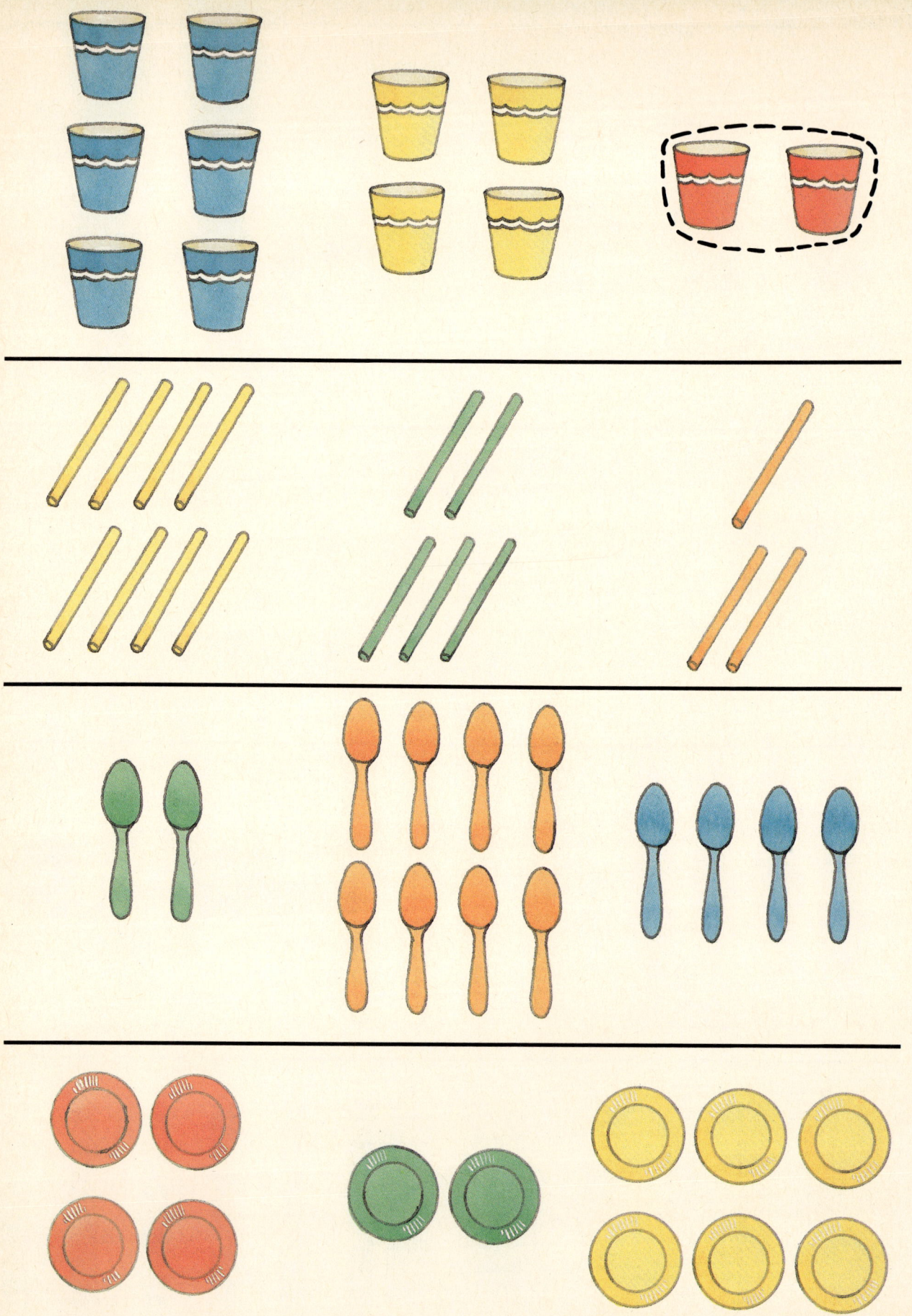

46 (forty-six) Recognizing fewest

Name _____

Recognizing the same number of objects **(forty-seven)** 47

48 (forty-eight) Practice

Name _____

Recognizing when one group has one more (forty-nine) 49

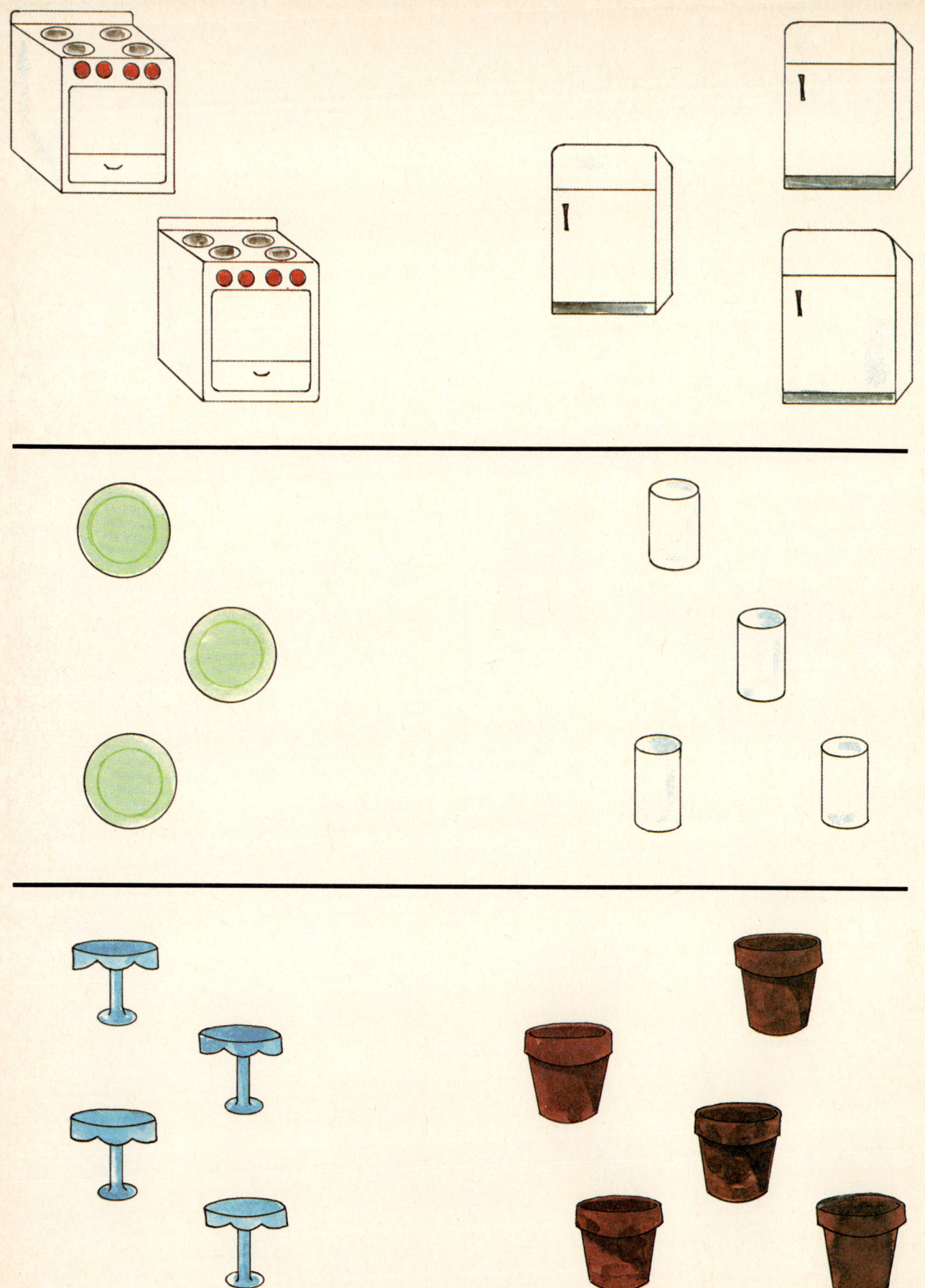

50 (fifty) Practice

Name _____

Activity: Drawing pictures in a specified order **(fifty-one)** 51

52 (fifty-two) Chapter 3 Evaluation

Chapter 4

Problem Formulation: Telling a story about a situation (fifty-three) 53

54 (fifty-four) Number readiness; one, two, and three

Name _____

Identifying first and next (sixty-three) 63

64 (sixty-four) Identifying second

Name _____

Identifying third **(sixty-five)** 65

66 (sixty-six) Identifying first, second, and third

Name _____

(1)   2   1   2

1   2   1   2

2   3    2   3

Recognizing how many pennies **(sixty-seven)**

1

2

3

1 2	1 2
2 3	2 3

68 (sixty-eight) Chapter 4 Evaluation

Chapter 5

Problem Formulation: Formulating puzzle questions (sixty-nine) 69

Recognizing 4

Name _____

4

5

5

Recognizing 5 (seventy-three) 73

5

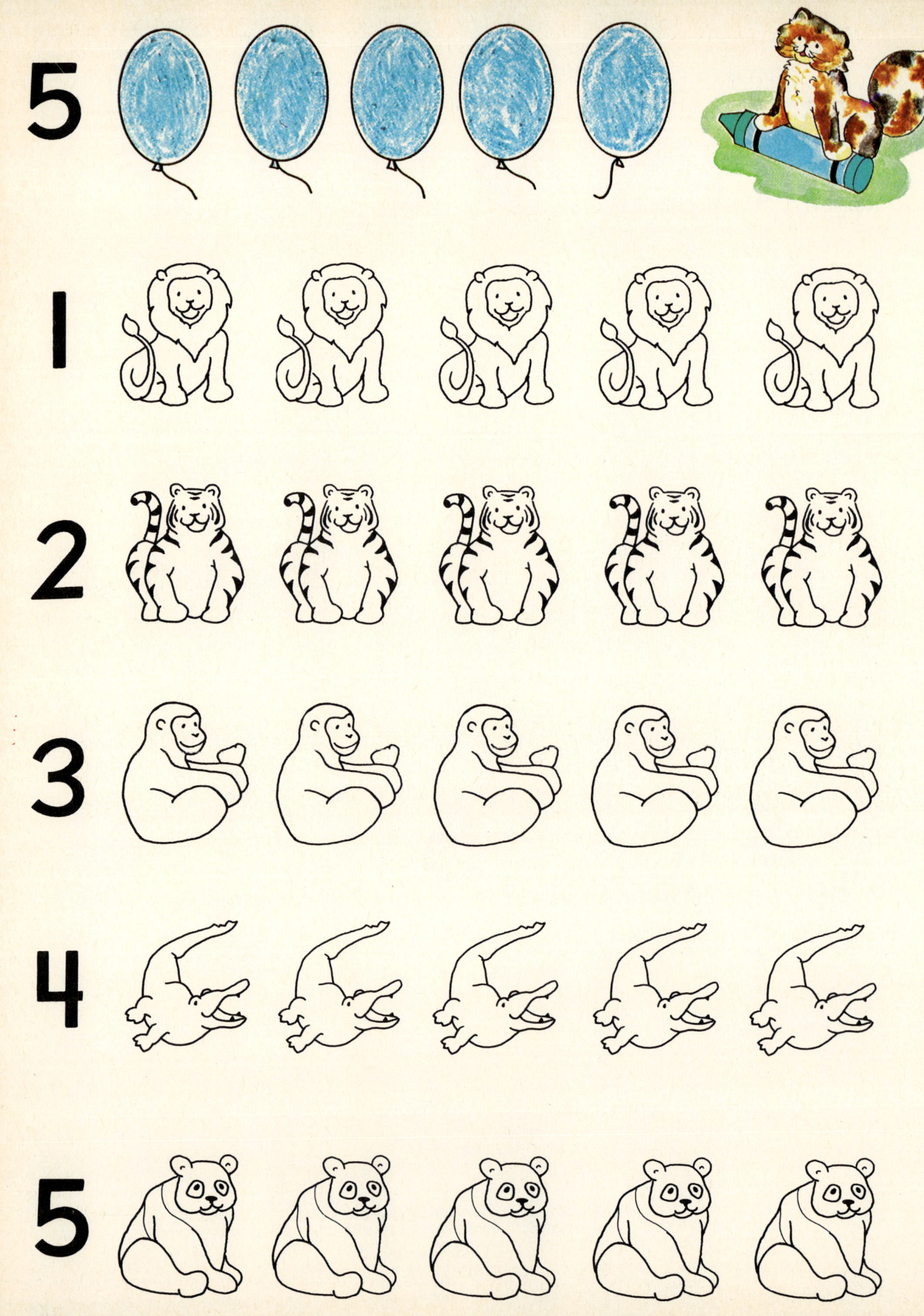

1

2

3

4

5

74 (seventy-four) Practice: Coloring how many to 5

Name _____

Writing 5 **(seventy-five)** 75

76 (seventy-six) Ordering to 5

Name _____

5

6

6

Recognizing 6 (seventy-seven) 77

1
2
3
4
5
6

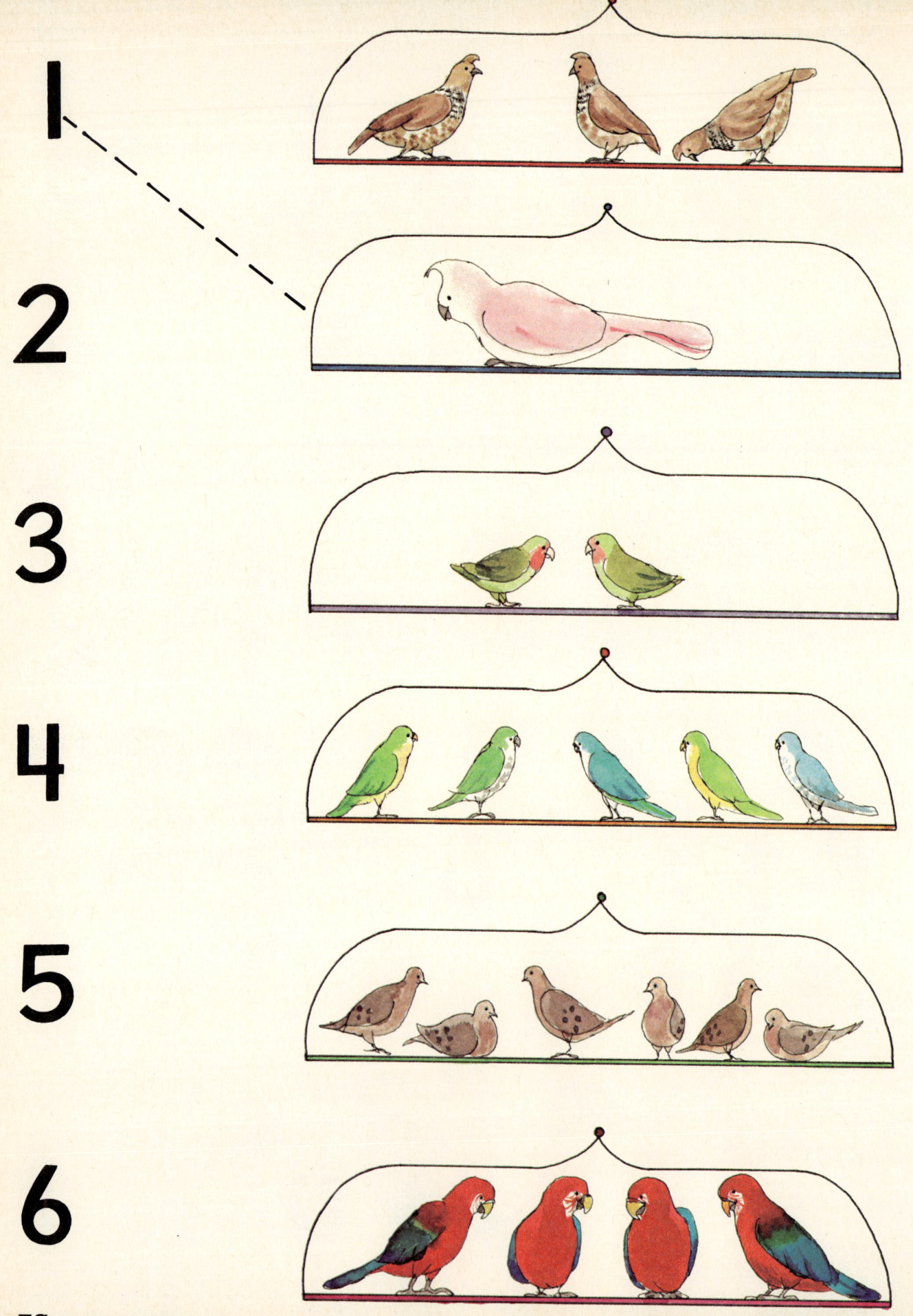

78 (seventy-eight) Counting how many to 6

Name _____

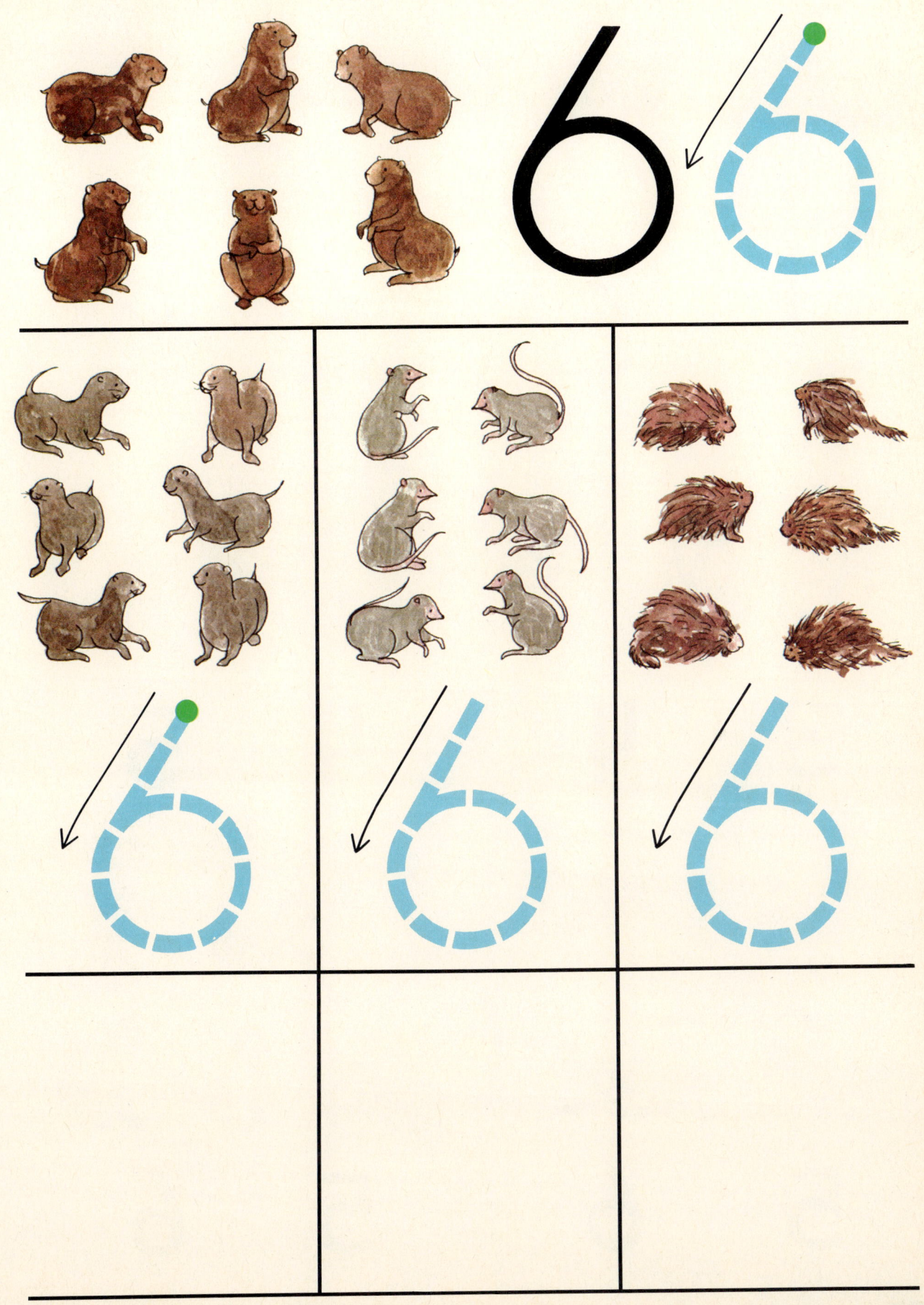

Writing 6 **(seventy-nine)** 79

1 ②   2 3

3 4   4 5

5 6   5 6

80 (eighty) Counting how many to 6

Name _____

0
1

Recognizing 0 (eighty-one) 81

82 (eighty-two) Writing 0

Name _____

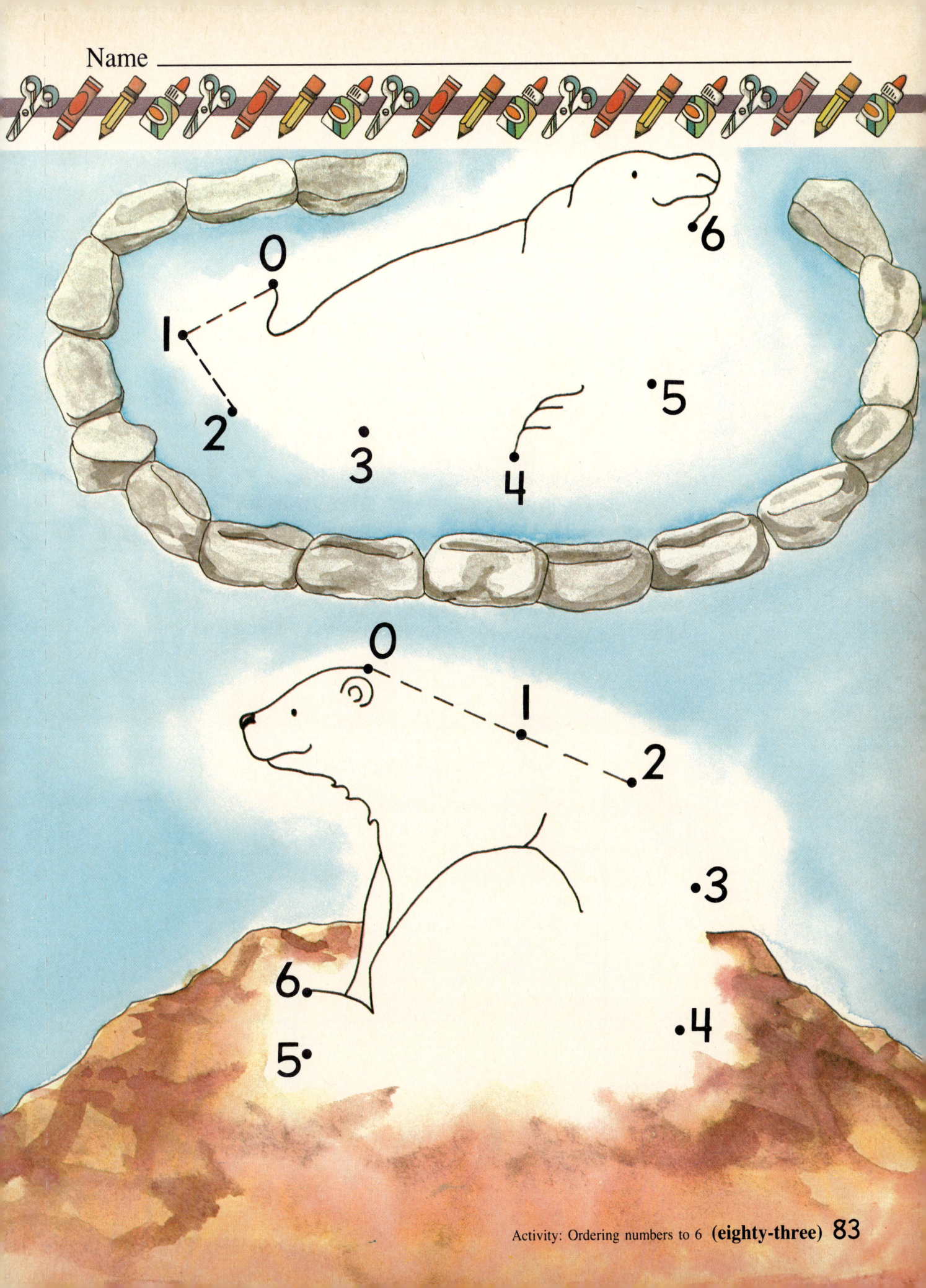

Activity: Ordering numbers to 6 (eighty-three) 83

4

5

6

4 3   5 4   5 6

0

84 (eighty-four) Chapter 5 Evaluation

Chapter 6

Problem Formulation: Formulating puzzle problems (eighty-five) 85

6
7

7

86 (eighty-six) Recognizing 7

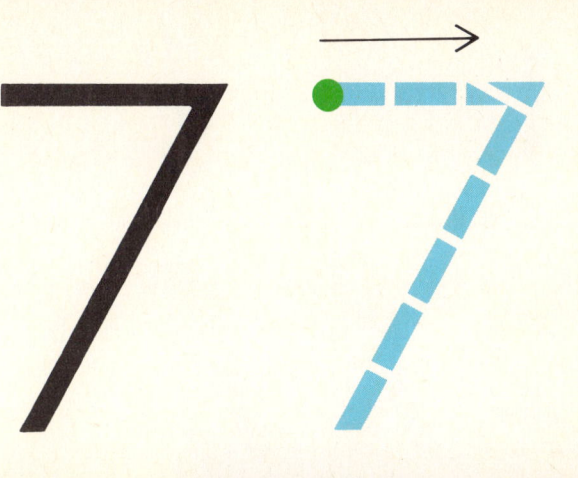

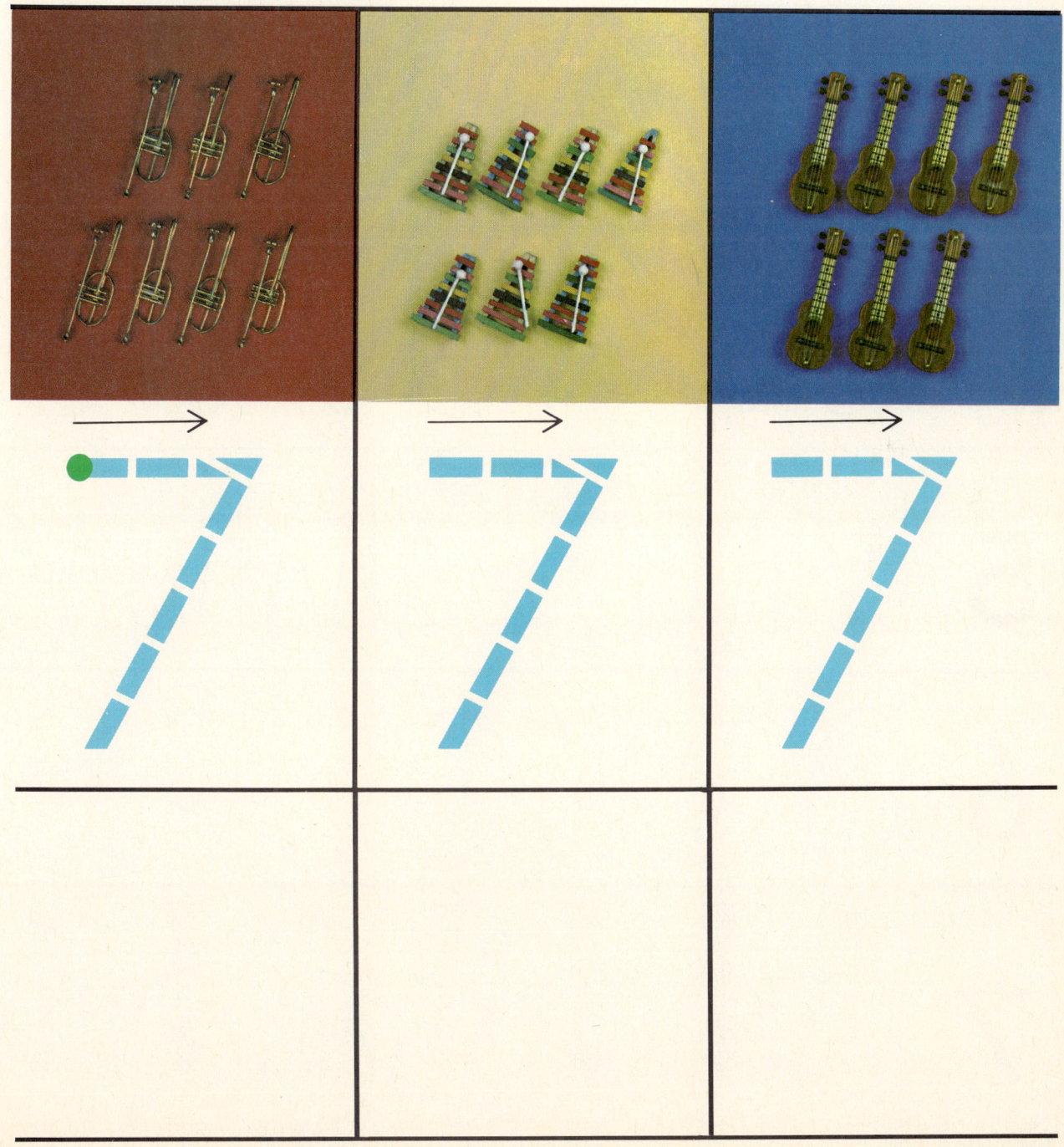

Name _____

Writing 7 (eighty-seven) 87

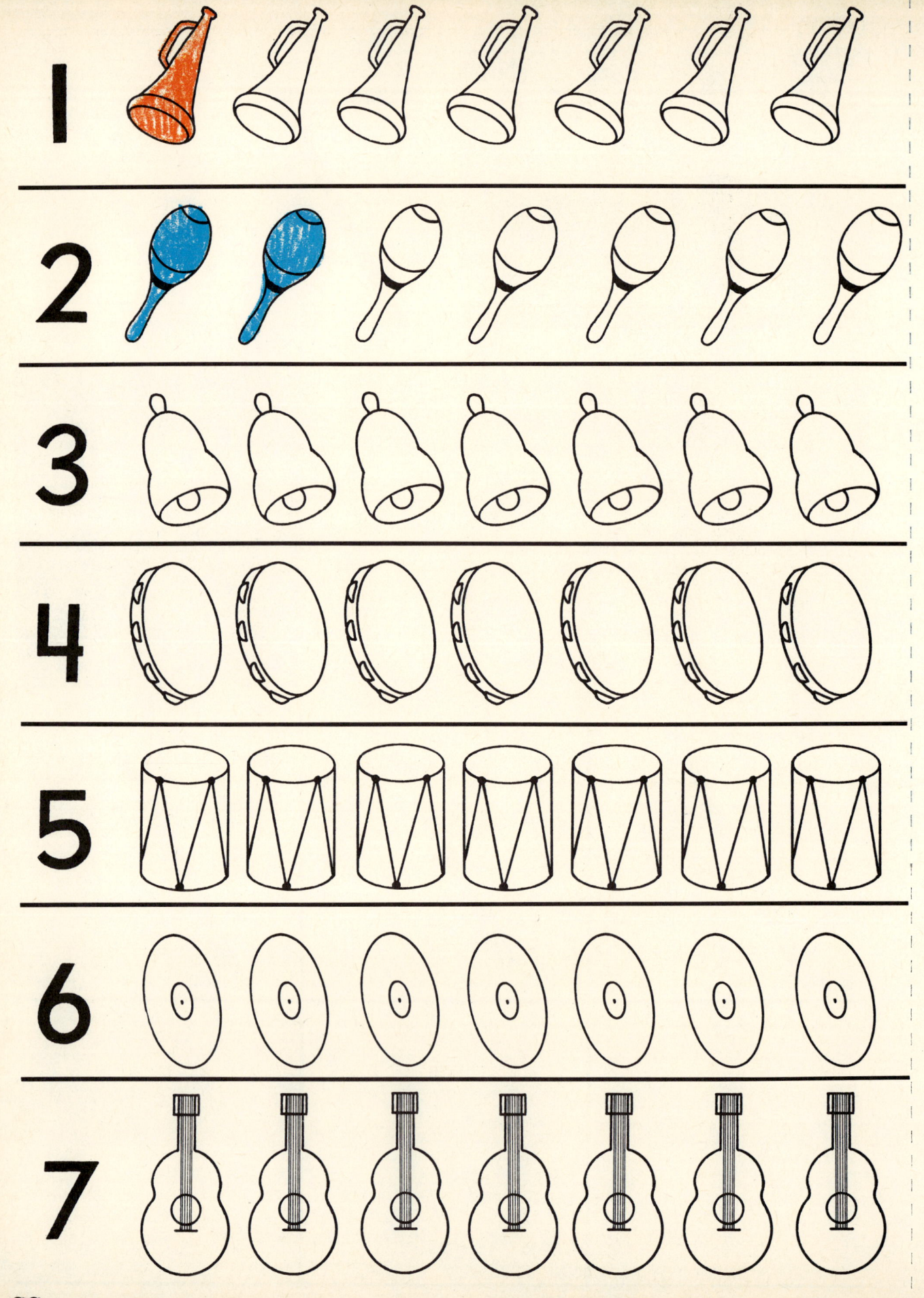

88 (eighty-eight) Coloring how many to 7

Name _____

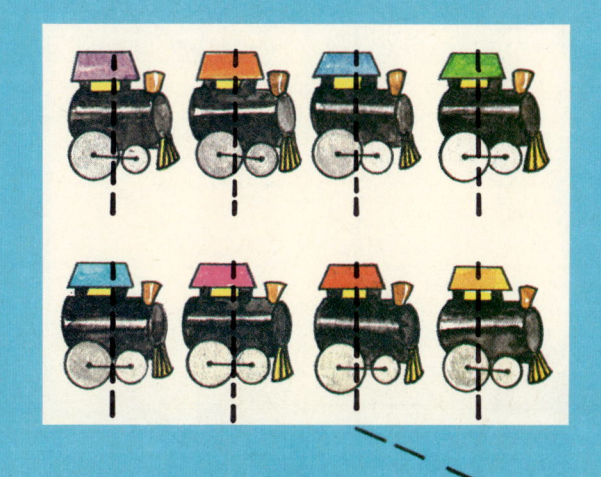

7

8

8

Recognizing 8 (eighty-nine) 89

8 7 8 7

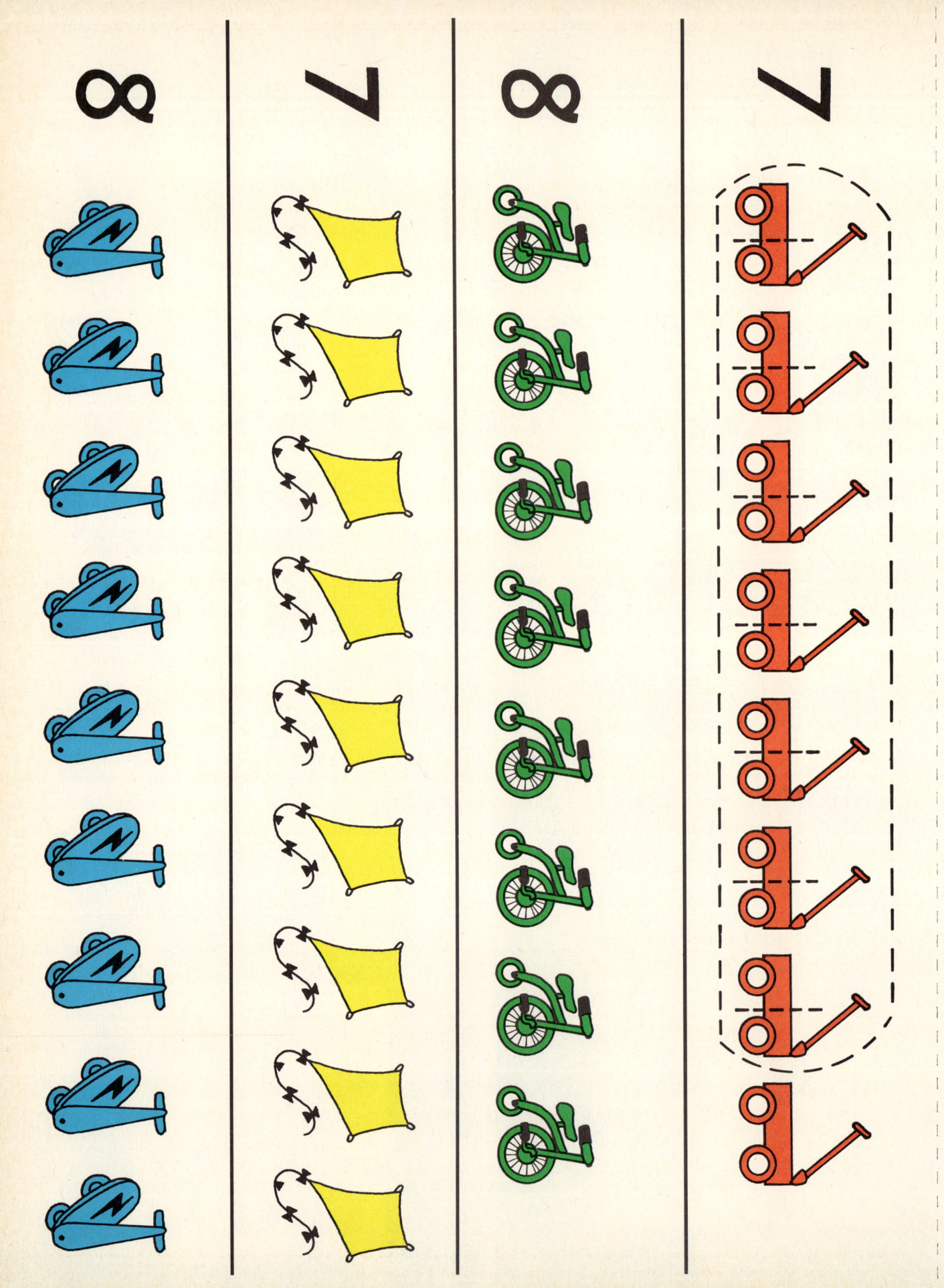

90 (ninety) Counting how many to 8

Name _____

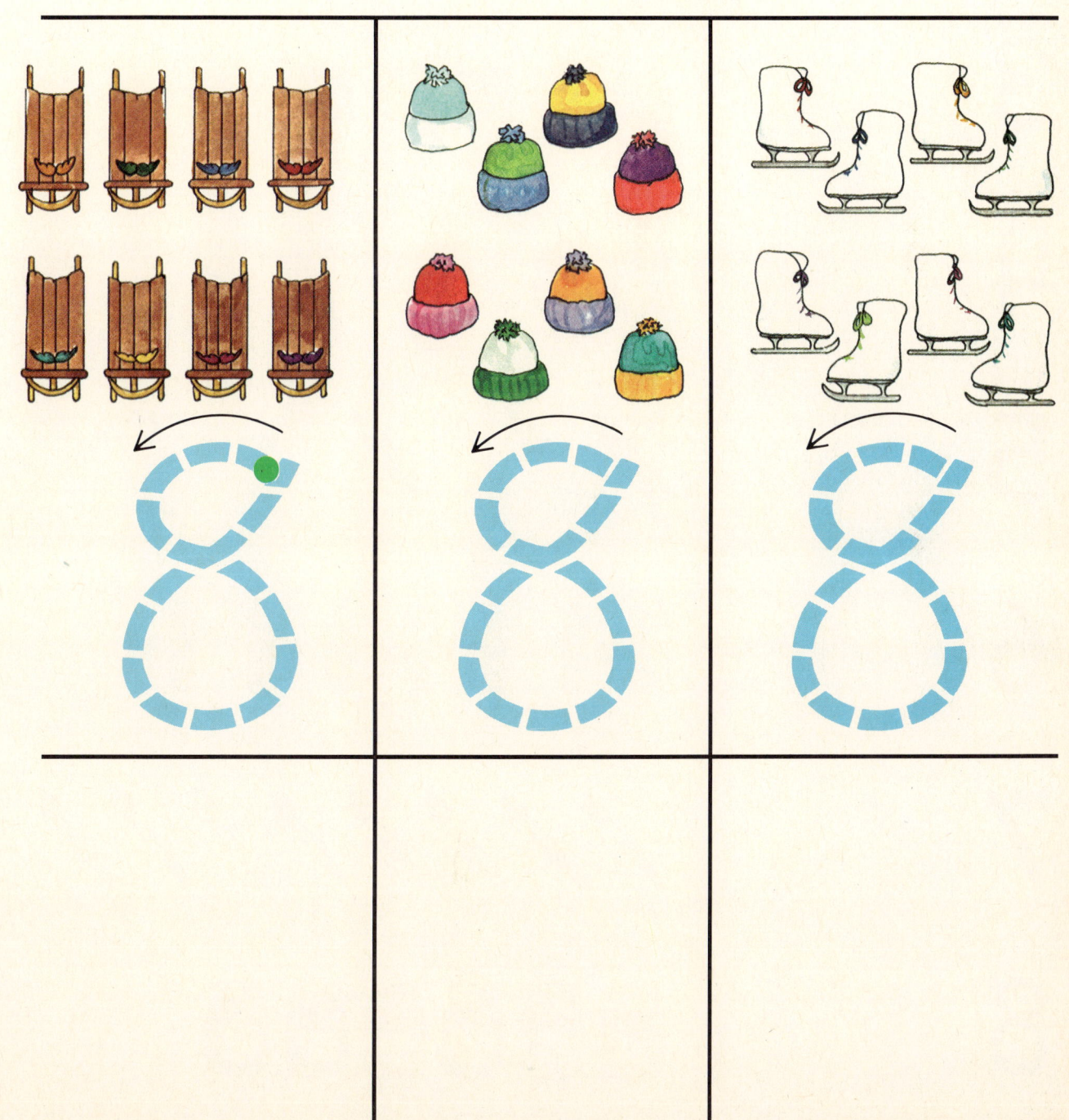

Writing 8 (ninety-one) 91

1
2
3
4
5
6
7
8

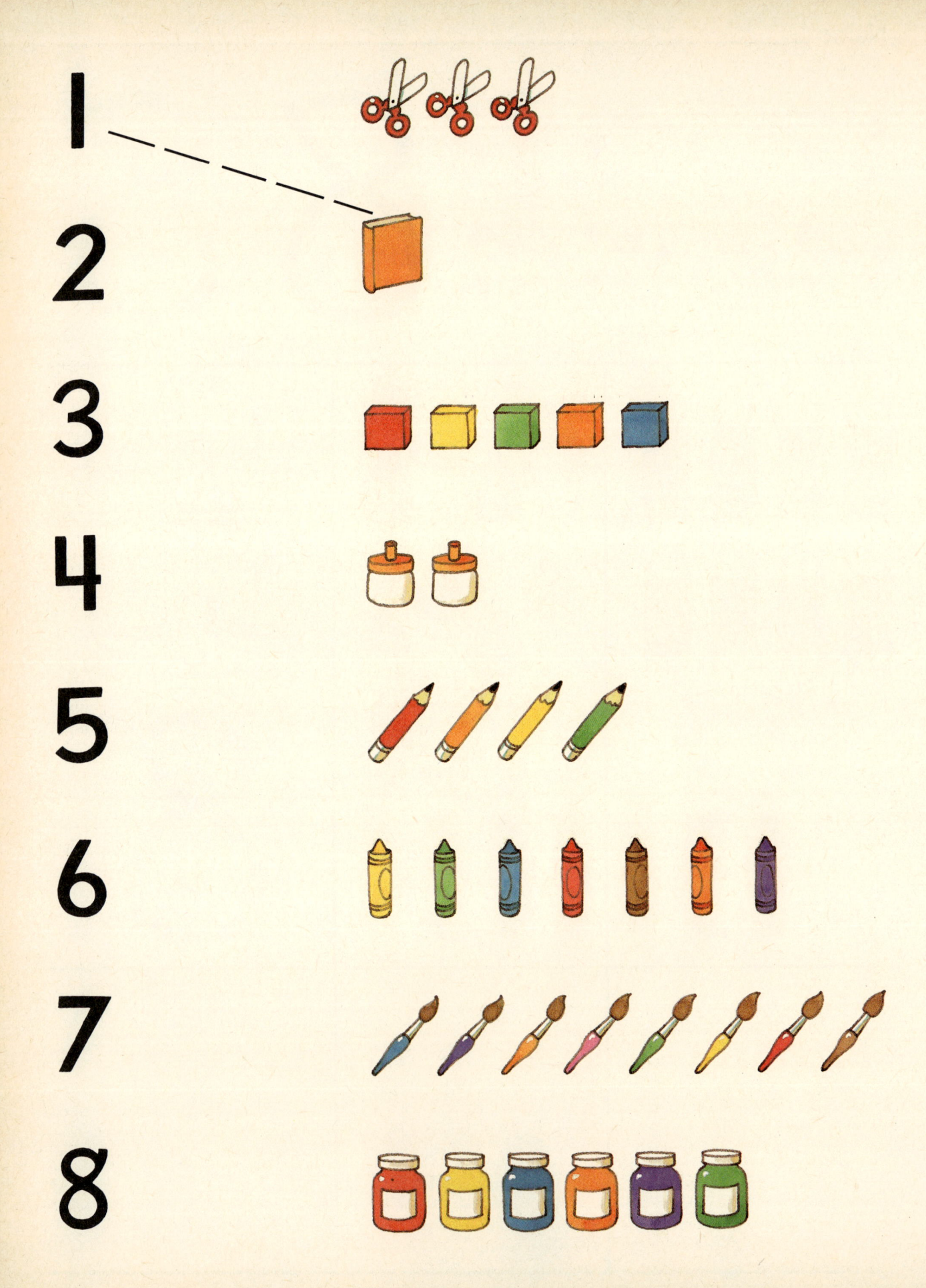

92 (ninety-two) Matching how many to 8

Name _____

8

9

9

Recognizing 9 (**ninety-three**) 93

94 (ninety-four) Practice

Name _____

Writing 9 (ninety-five) 95

96 (ninety-six) Ordering to 9

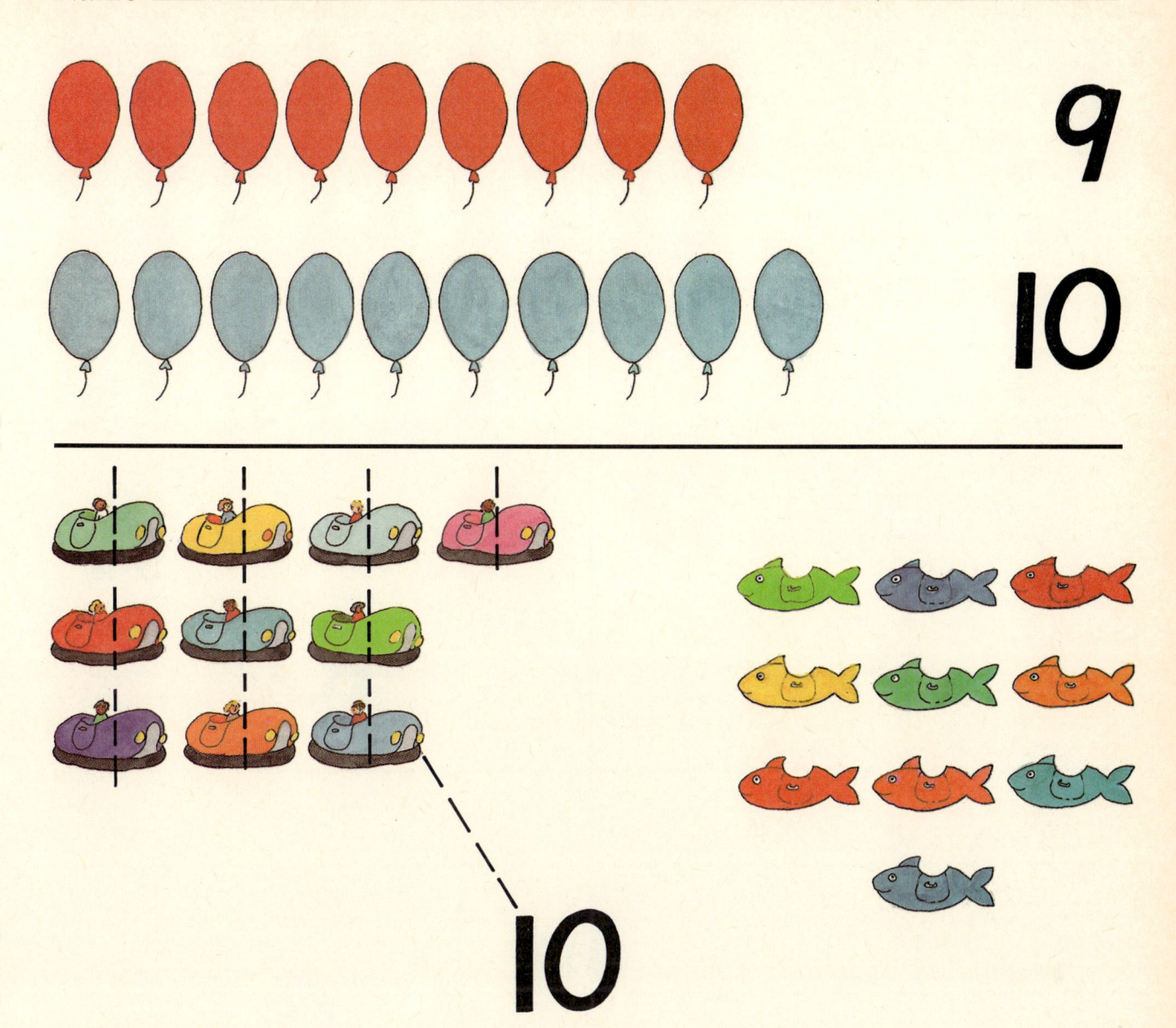

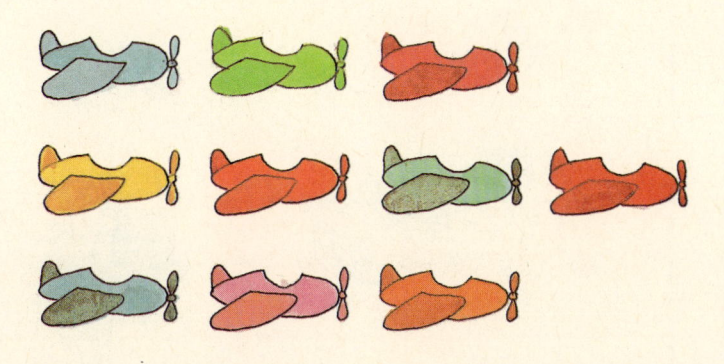

Name _____

9

10

10

Recognizing 10 (ninety-seven) 97

9

10

9

10

98 (ninety-eight) Counting to 10

Name _____

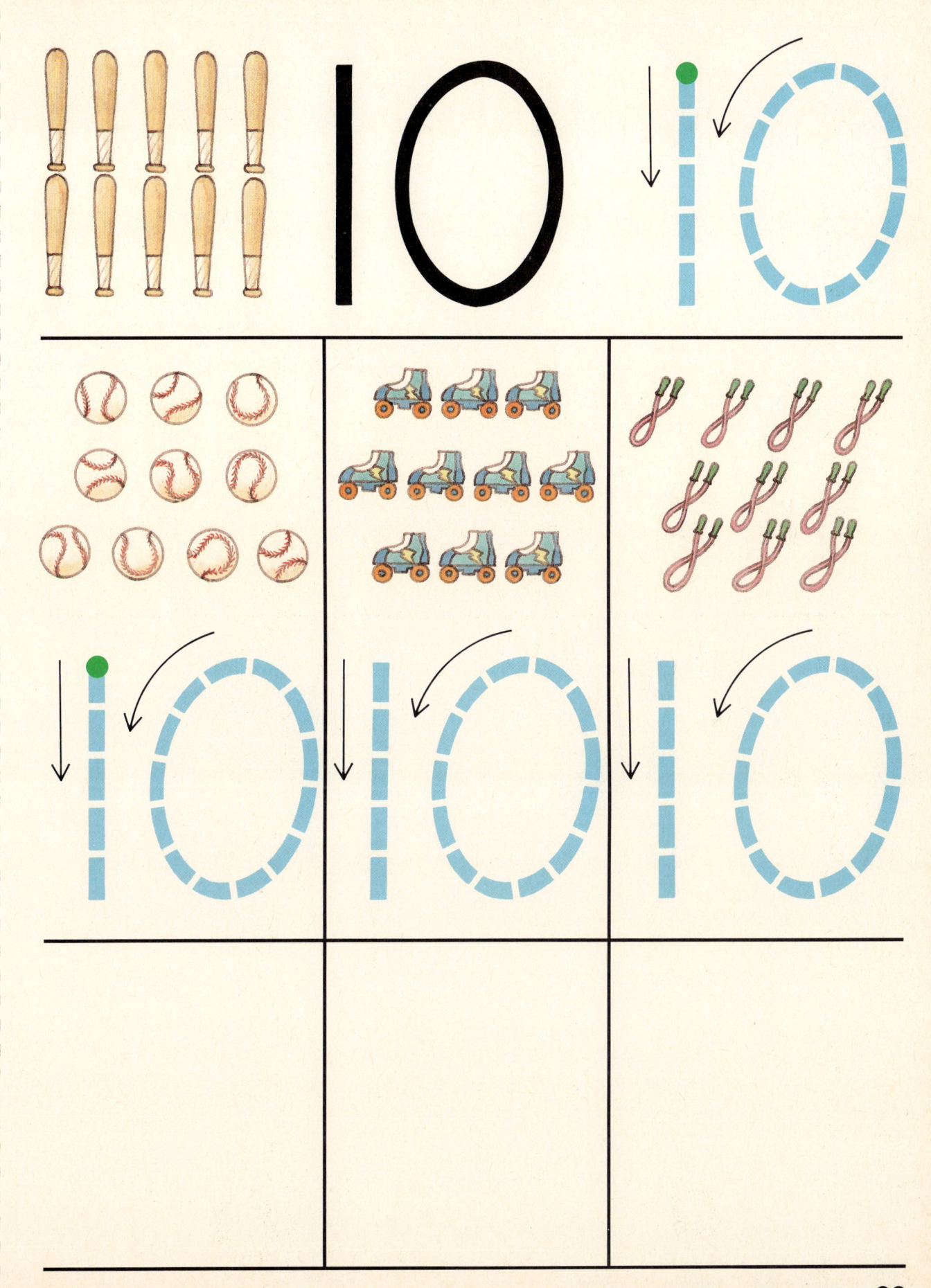

Writing 10 (ninety-nine) 99

100 **(one hundred)** Activity: Ordering numbers from 0 to 10

Name _____

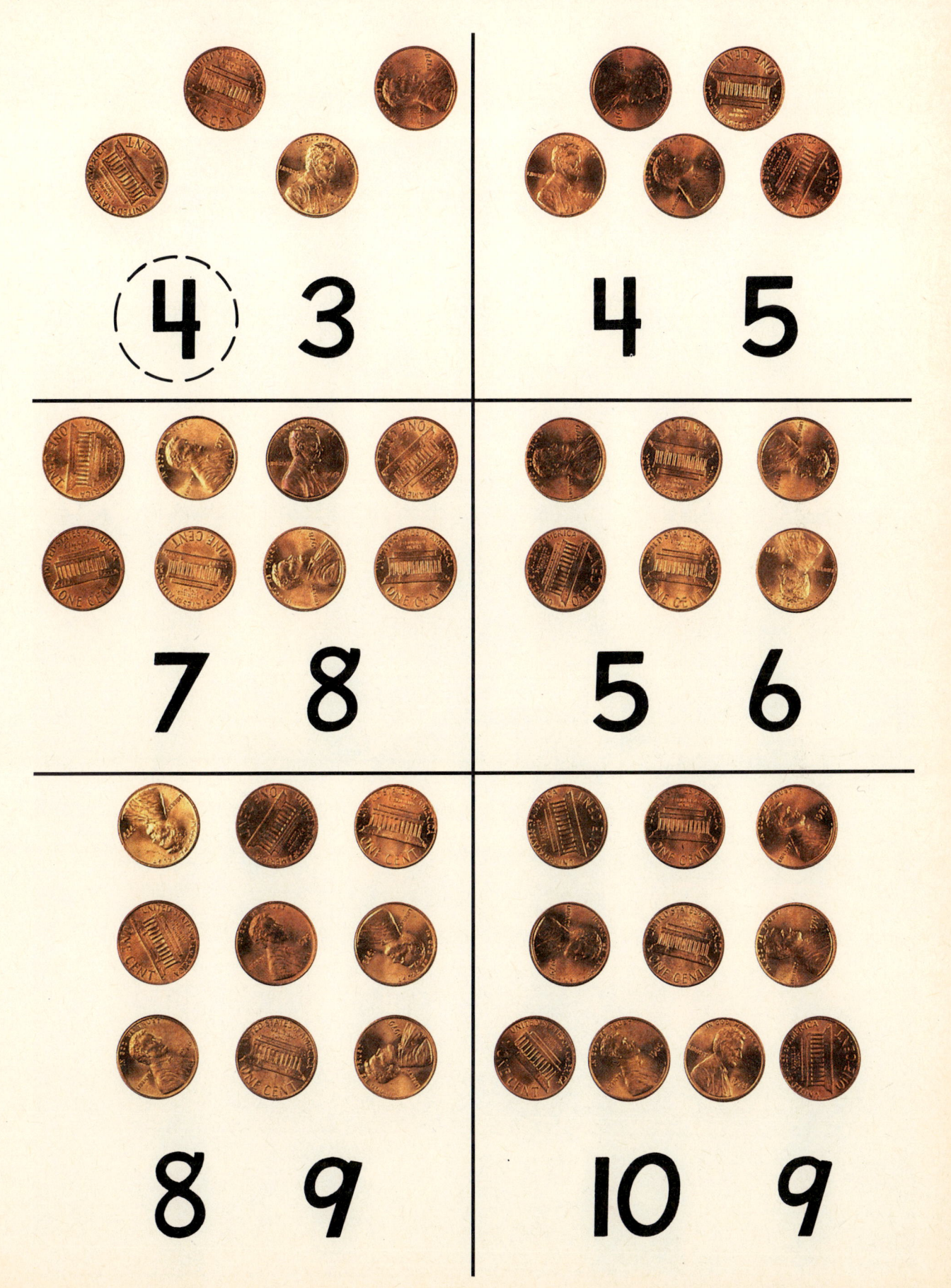

(4) 3

4 5

7 8

5 6

8 9

10 9

Counting to 10 (one hundred one) 101

102 (one hundred two) Activity: Completing a picture puzzle; Computer

Name _____

7

8

9

10

8

---

7 6 | 9 10

Chapter 6 Evaluation (one hundred three) 103

104 (one hundred four) Maintenance: Concepts

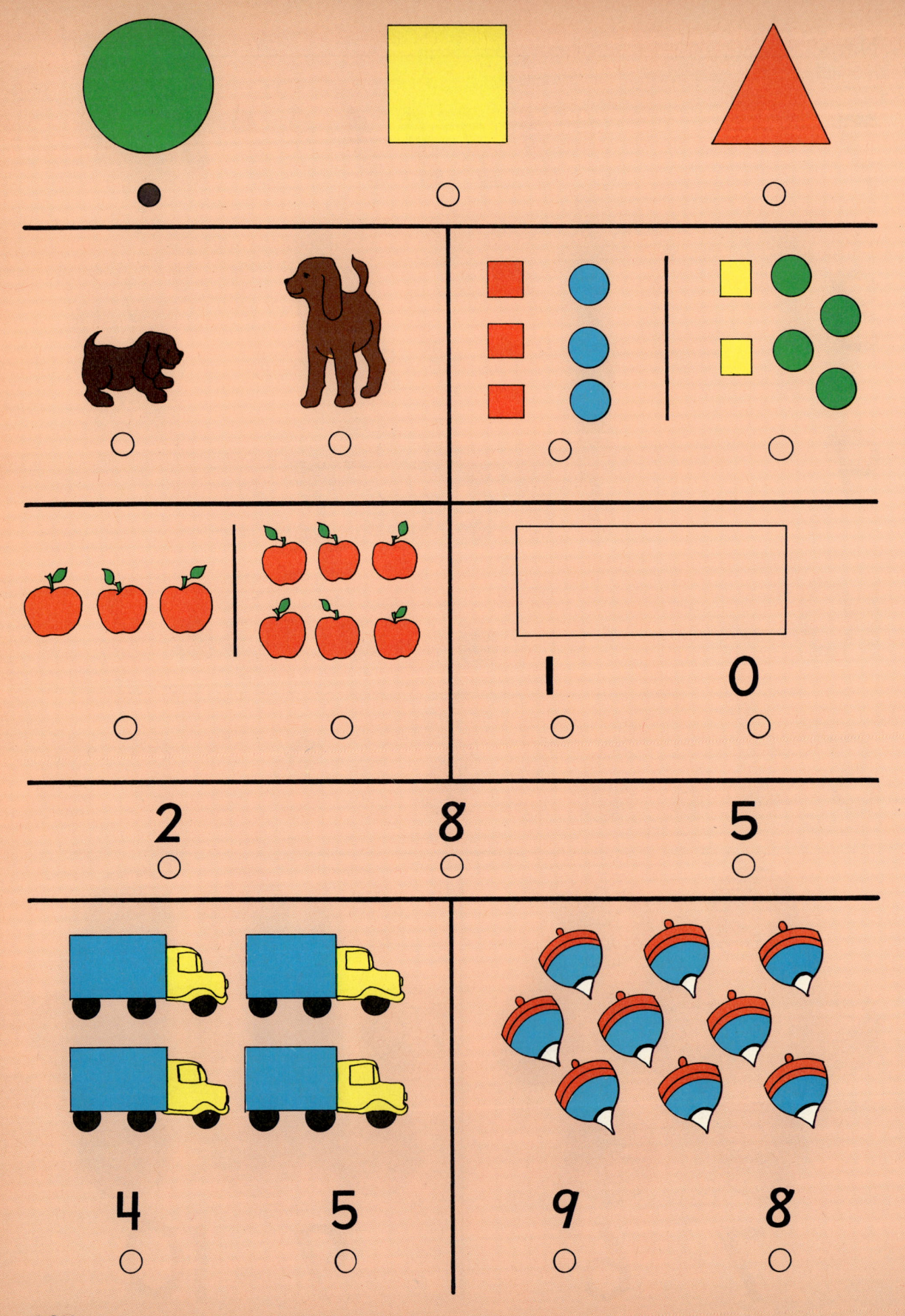

Chapter 7

BACK TO SCHOOL SUPPLIES

Problem Formulation: Telling a story about a situation **(one hundred five)** 105

106 (one hundred six) Recognizing the order of events

Name _____

Identifying daytime activities (one hundred seven) 107

108 (one hundred eight) Identifying nighttime activities

Name _____

Telling which takes more time (one hundred nine) 109

110 (one hundred ten) Telling which takes the most time

Name _____

1¢

1¢   2¢   2¢   3¢

3¢   4¢   5¢   6¢

Recognizing the value of a penny **(one hundred eleven)** 111

4¢   (5¢)

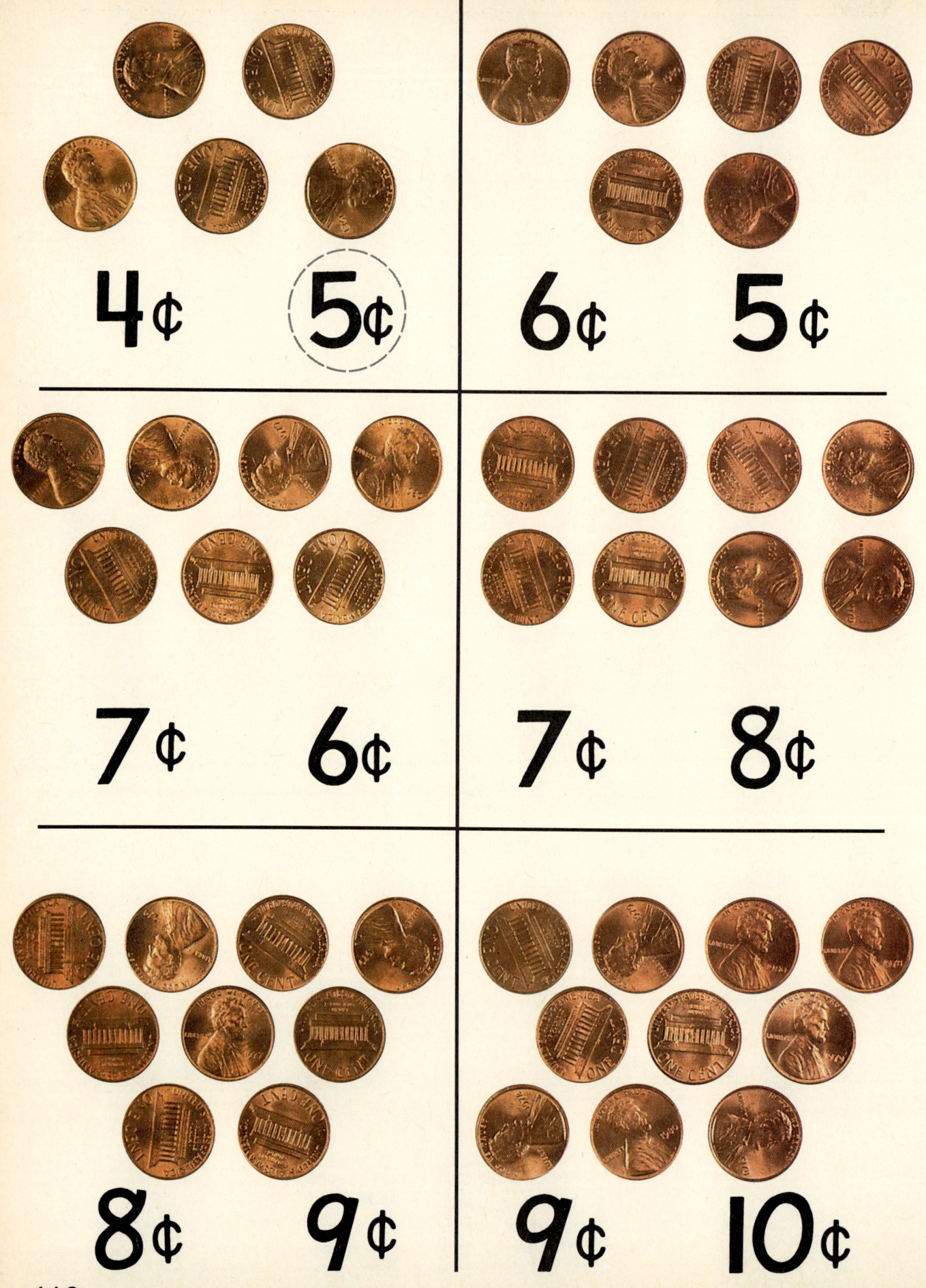

6¢   5¢

7¢   6¢

7¢   8¢

8¢   9¢

9¢   10¢

112 (one hundred twelve) Practice

Name _____

5¢   5¢

5¢

Recognizing the value of a nickel **(one hundred thirteen)** 113

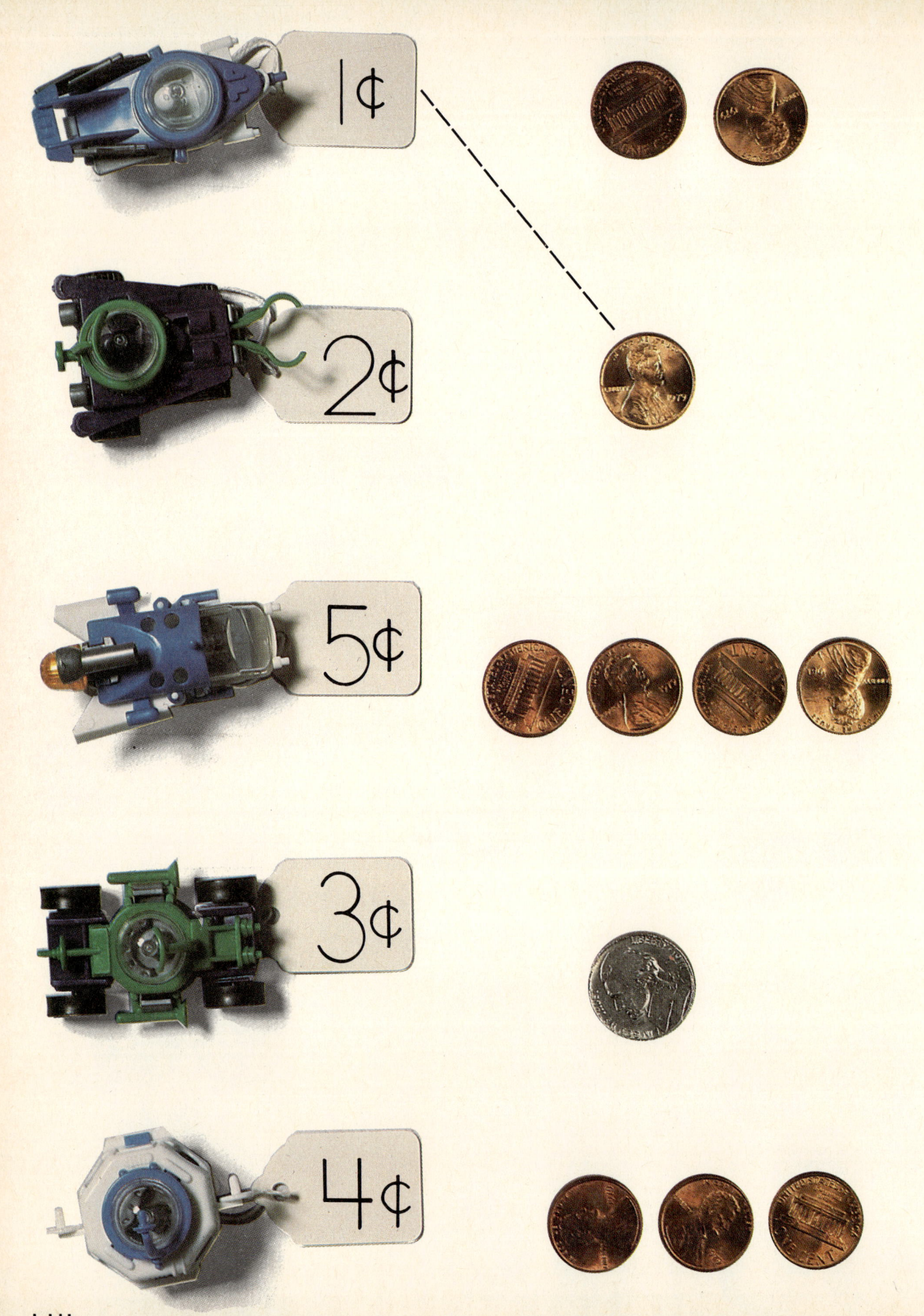

114 (one hundred fourteen) Practice

Name _____

10¢   10¢   10¢

Recognizing the value of a dime (one hundred fifteen) 115

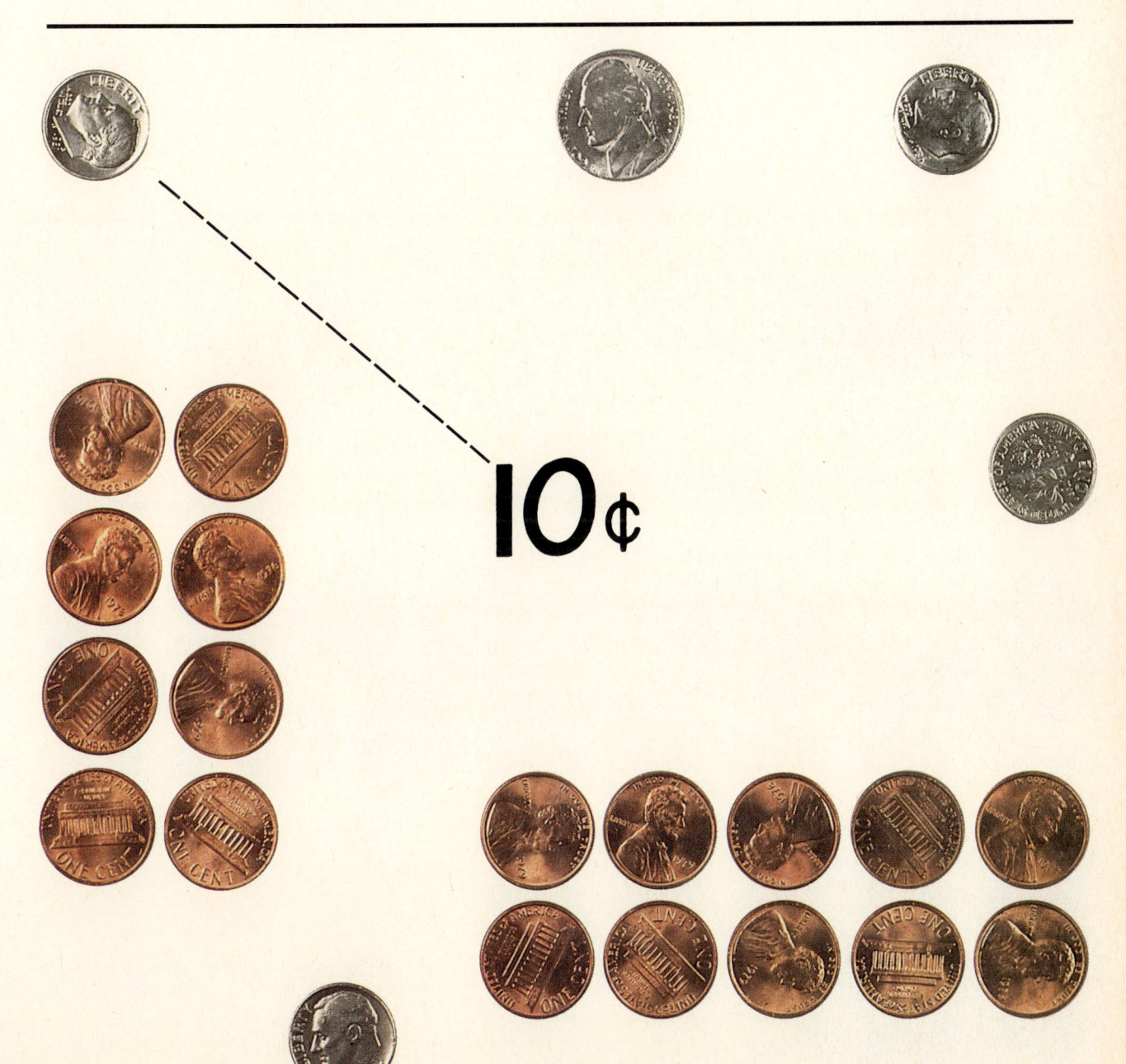

116 (one hundred sixteen) Practice

Name _____

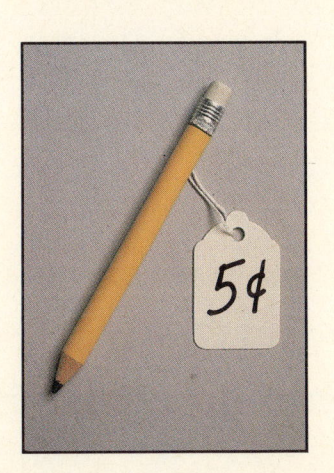

Showing 5 and 10 cents two ways (one hundred seventeen) 117

10¢
1¢
5¢

118 (one hundred eighteen) Chapter 7 Evaluation

Chapter 8

Problem Formulation: Telling a story suggesting the joining of two sets

1   1   2
---
2   1   3
---
3   1   4

120 (one hundred twenty) Telling how many in each group and in all

Name _____

2   1   3

3   1   4

4   1   5

Telling how many in each group and in all (one hundred twenty-one) 121

1   2   3

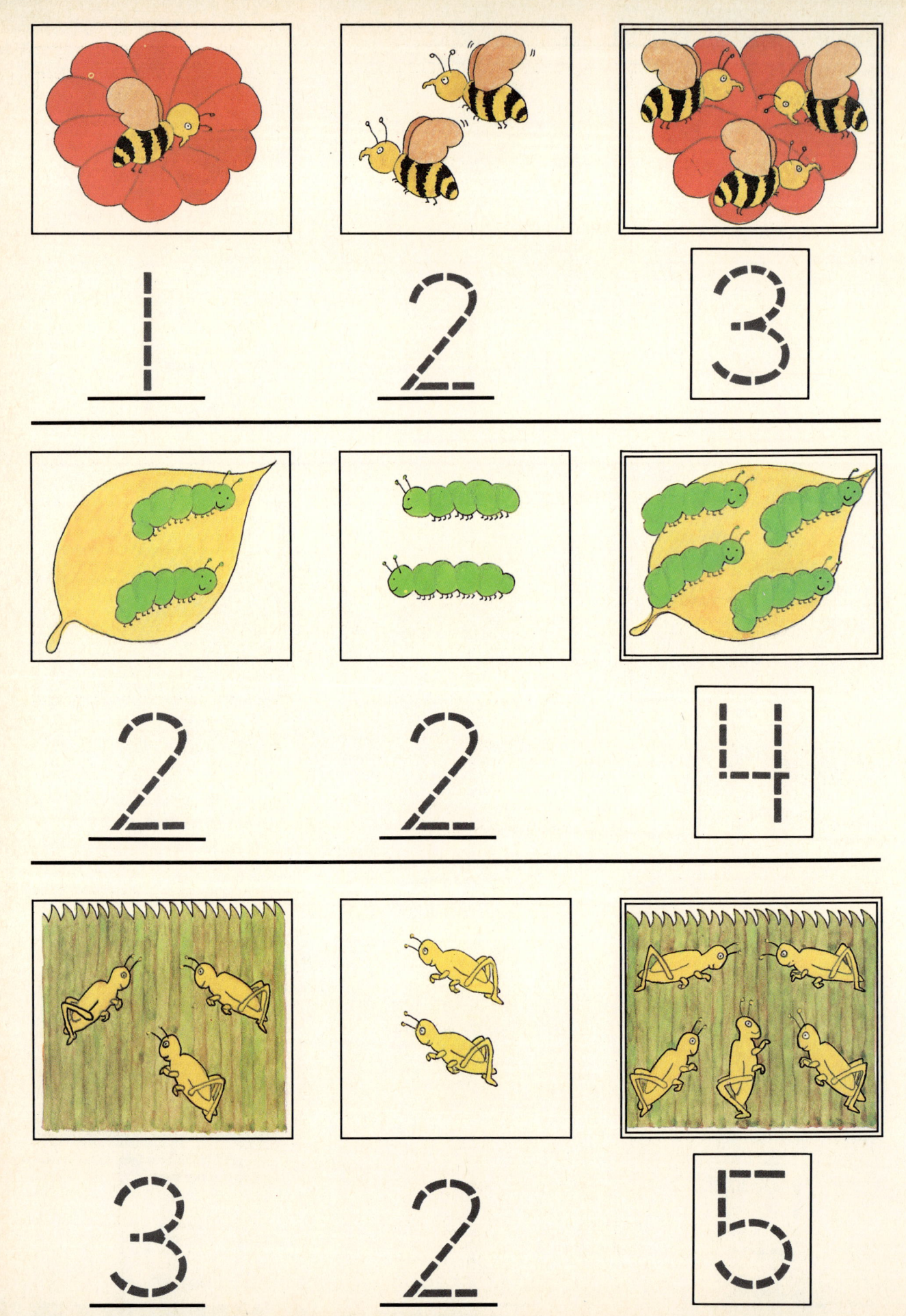

2   2   4

3   2   5

122 (one hundred twenty-two) Practice

Name _____

2 + 1 = 3

4 + 1 =

2 + 2 =

Introducing the plus sign **(one hundred twenty-three)** 123

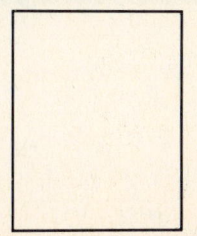

1 + 4

3 + 3

2 + 4

124 (one hundred twenty-four) Practice

Name _____

```
  1          1
+ 2        + 3
---        ---
  3
```

```
  2          2
+ 1        + 2
---        ---
```

Addition facts to 6 **(one hundred twenty-five)** 125

1
+4
___

3
+3
___

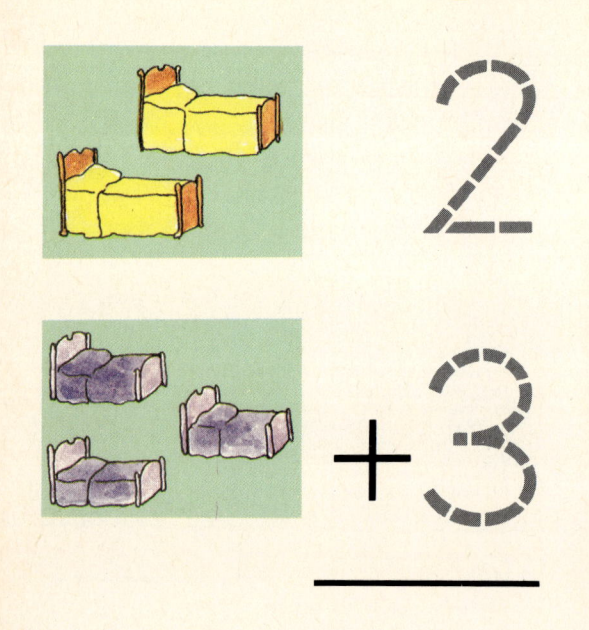

2
+3
___

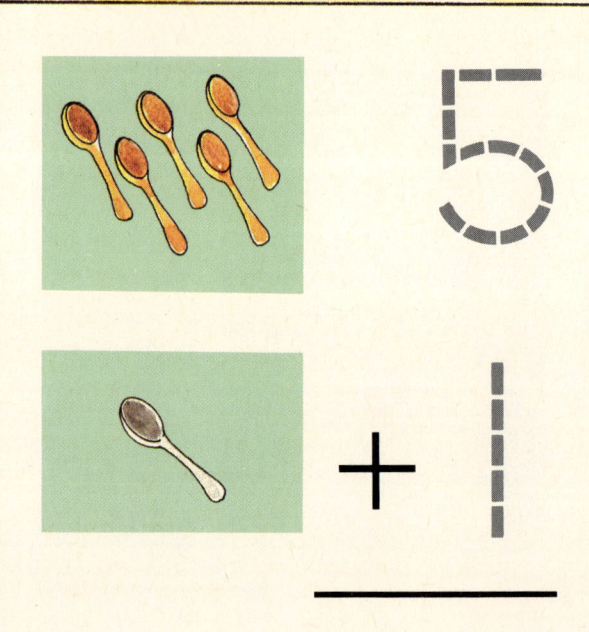

5
+1
___

126 (one hundred twenty-six) Practice

Name _____

     1   2
    +1   +1
    ──   ──
     2

     3   4
    +1   +1
    ──   ──

Addition facts to 6 (one hundred twenty-seven) 127

2
+2
___

1
+4
___

5
+1
___

4
+2
___

128 (one hundred twenty-eight) Practice

Name _____

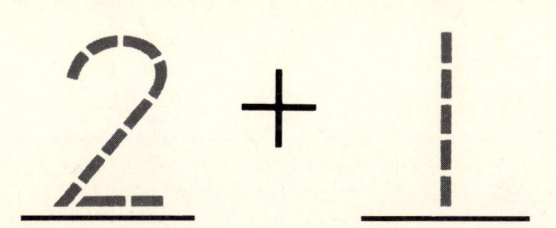

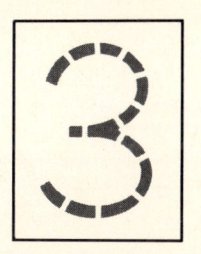

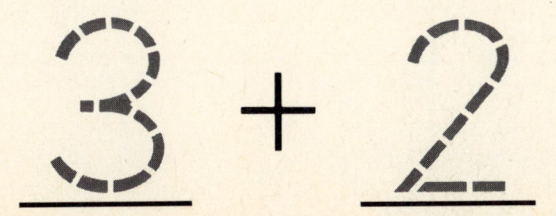

2 + 1 = 3

3 + 1 = ☐

3 + 2 = ☐

Problem Solving: Solving pictured problems (one hundred twenty-nine) 129

2 + 1 = ☐

3 + 2 = ☐

3
+1
___

2
+4
___

130 (one hundred thirty) Chapter 8 Evaluation

Chapter 9

Problem Formulation: Telling a story suggesting the separation of sets **(one hundred thirty-one)** 131

2 − 1 = 1

3 − 1 = 2

4 − 1 = 3

132 (one hundred thirty-two) Telling how many in all, taken away, and left

Name _____

3   1   2

5   1   4

4   2   2

Telling how many in all, going away, and left **(one hundred thirty-three)** 133

3   2   1

4   3   1

5   4   1

134 (one hundred thirty-four) Practice

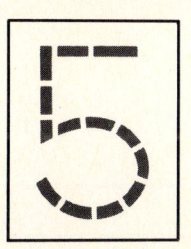

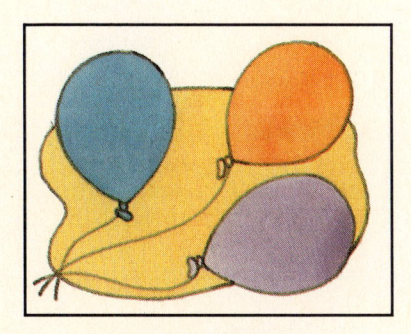

Name _____

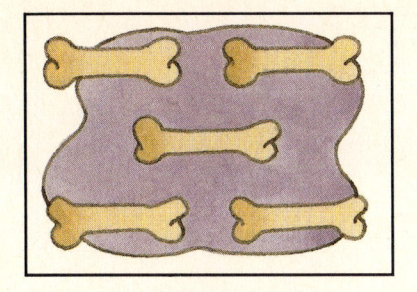

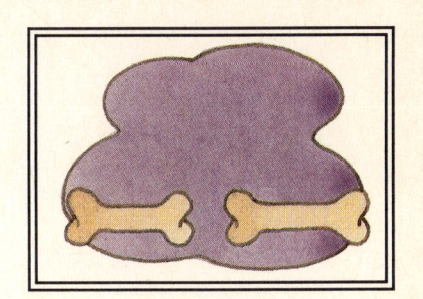

5 - 3 2

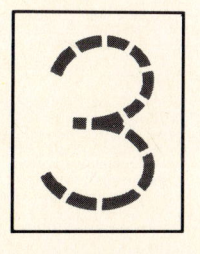

3 - 2 __

6 - 2 __

Showing how many are left (one hundred thirty-five) 135

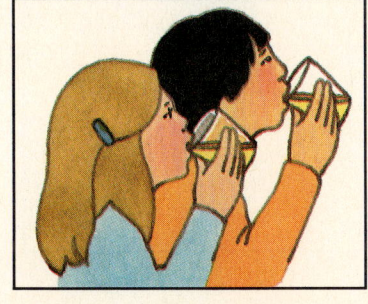

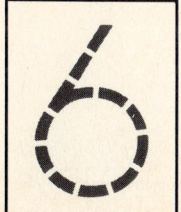

5 - 2 ___

6 - 4 ___

6 - 3 ___

136 (one hundred thirty-six) Practice

Name

Problem Solving: Telling stories for subtraction pictures **(one hundred thirty-seven)** 137

2 
3
4
5

1 + 1

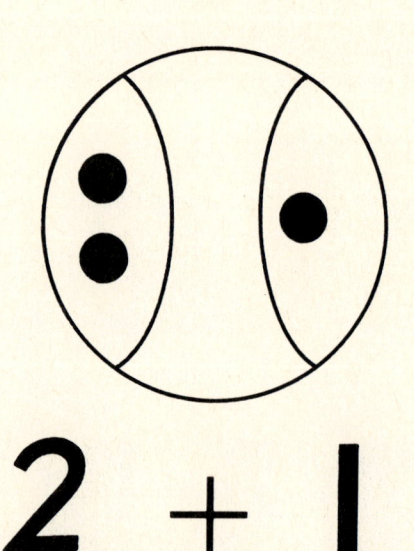

2 + 1

3 + 1

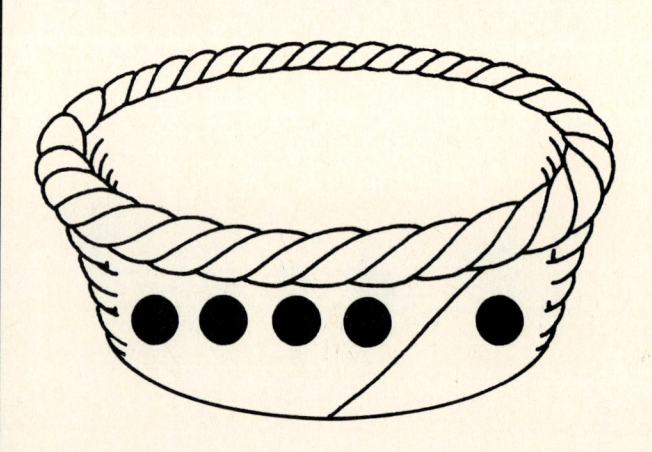

4 + 1

138 (one hundred thirty-eight) Activity: Addition

Name _____

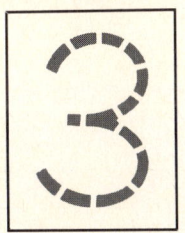

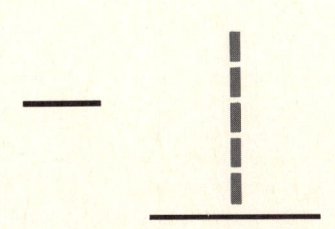

3 - 1 = __

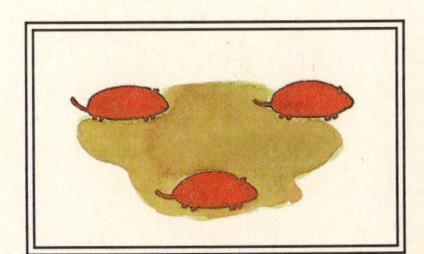

5 - 2 = __

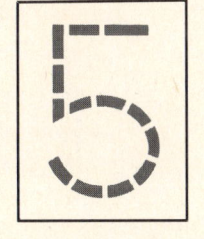

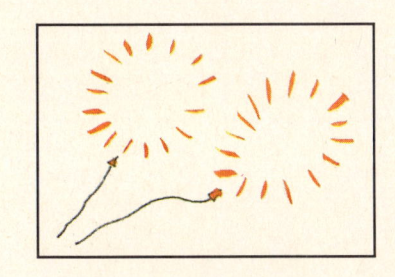

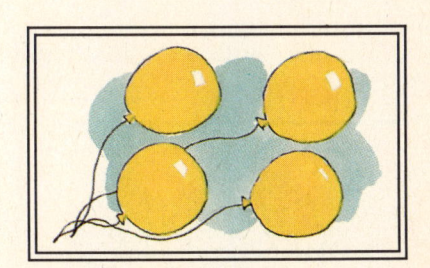

6 - 2 = __

Chapter 9 Evaluation (one hundred thirty-nine) 139

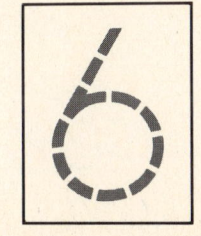

○ 8
○ 9
● 10

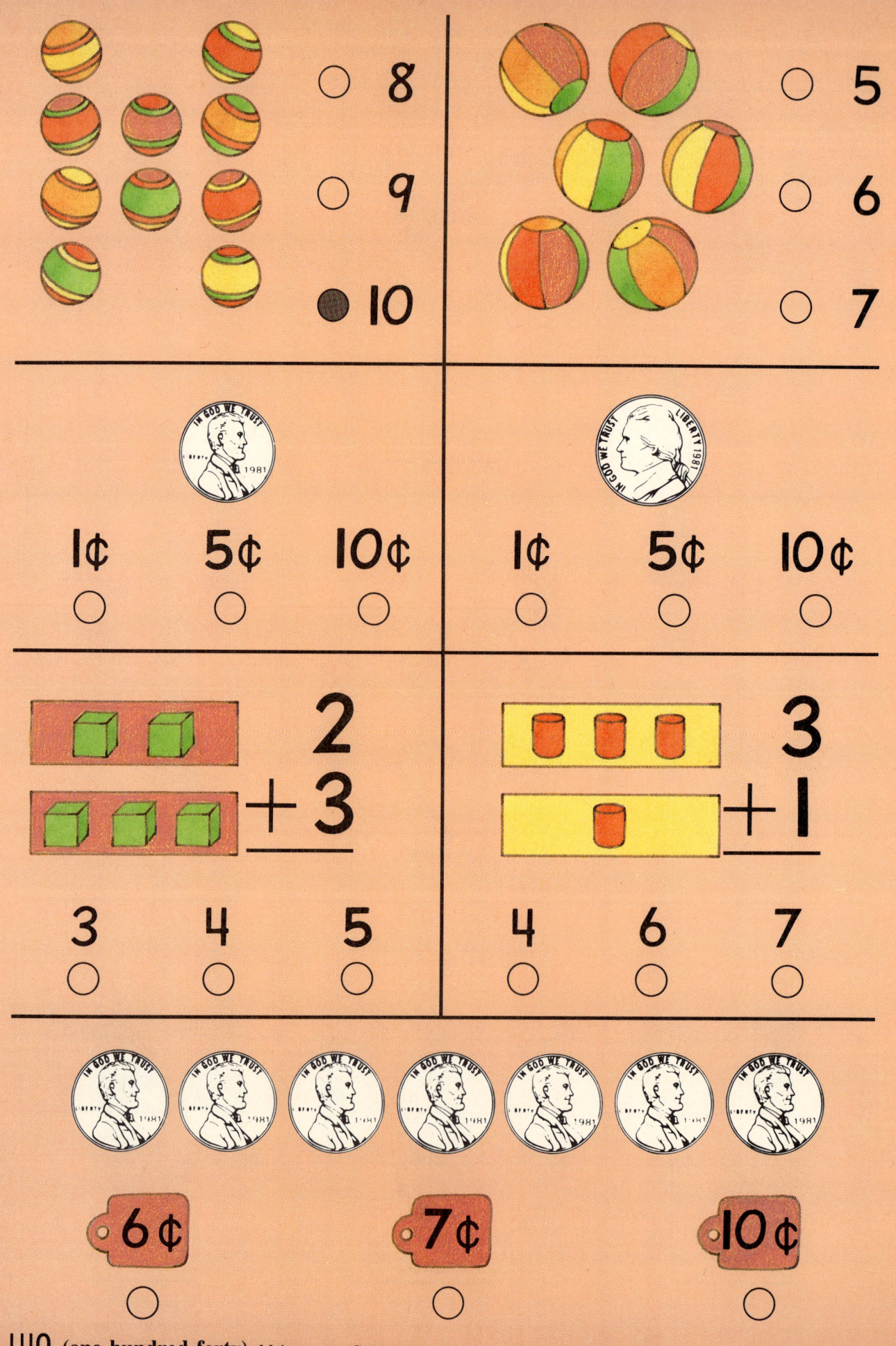

○ 5
○ 6
○ 7

1¢   5¢   10¢
○   ○   ○

1¢   5¢   10¢
○   ○   ○

2
+3
───
3   4   5
○   ○   ○

3
+1
───
4   6   7
○   ○   ○

6¢   7¢   10¢
○   ○   ○

140 (one hundred forty)   Maintenance: Concepts

Chapter 10

Problem Formulation: Formulating problems

142 (one hundred forty-two) Recognizing same-size parts

Name _____

Recognizing one half (one hundred forty-three) 143

144 (one hundred forty-four) Recognizing one third

Name _____

Recognizing one fourth **(one hundred forty-five)** 145

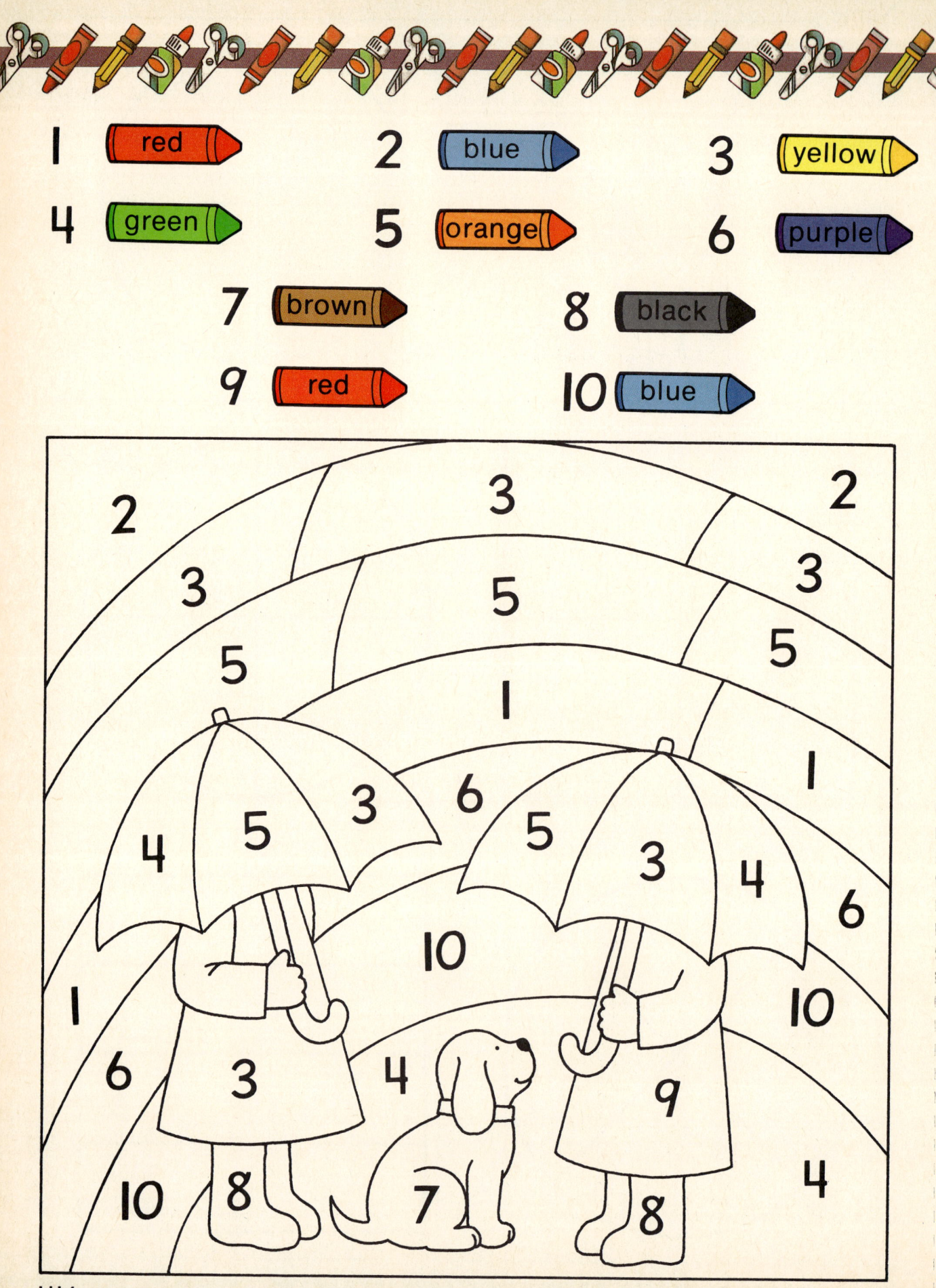

1 red 2 blue 3 yellow
4 green 5 orange 6 purple
7 brown 8 black
9 red 10 blue

146 (one hundred forty-six) Enrichment Activity: Coloring by number

Name _____

10

11

11

10

10

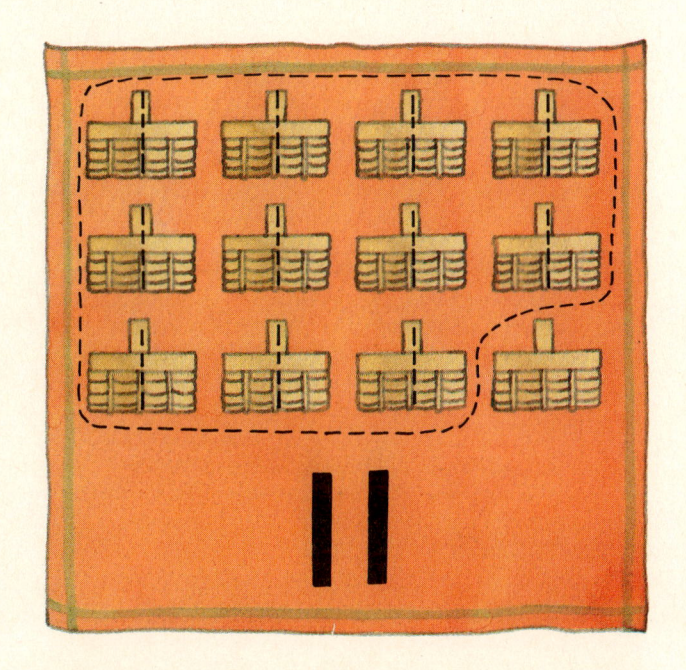

11

Recognizing 11 **(one hundred forty-seven)** 147

11

12

12

11

11

12

148 (one hundred forty-eight) Recognizing 12

Name _____

Reading a clock face **(one hundred forty-nine)** 149

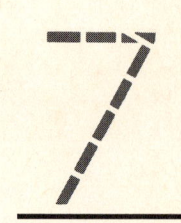

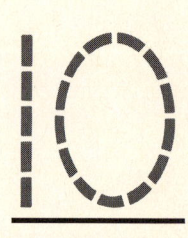

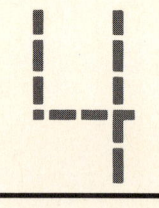

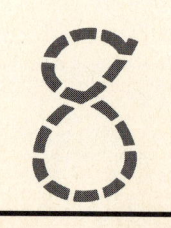

150 (one hundred fifty) Associating daily activities with time

Name _____

13

Counting to 13 **(one hundred fifty-one)** 151

14

152 (one hundred fifty-two) Counting to 14

Name _____

15

Counting to 15 (one hundred fifty-three) 153

16

154 (one hundred fifty-four) Counting to 16

Name _____

17

Counting to 17 (one hundred fifty-five) 155

18

156 (one hundred fifty-six) Counting to 18

Name _____

19

Counting to 19 (one hundred fifty-seven) 157

20

Name _____

0   20   19   18
1
2
3 4   15 16
5   14
6   13
7   12
8 9 10 11

Activity: Ordering numbers from 0 to 20; Computer **(one hundred fifty-nine)** 159

12

15
20

160 (one hundred sixty) Chapter 10 Evaluation

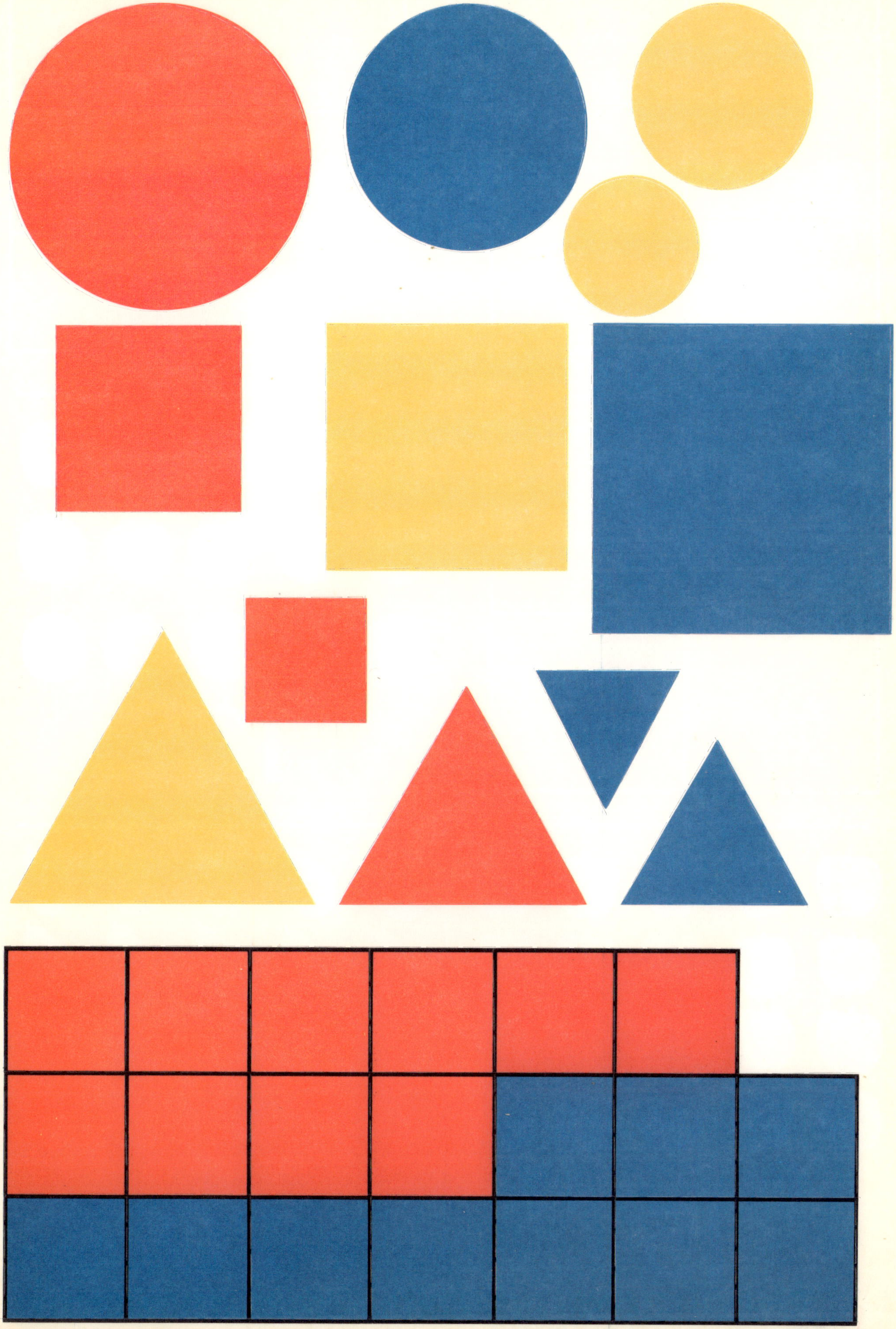

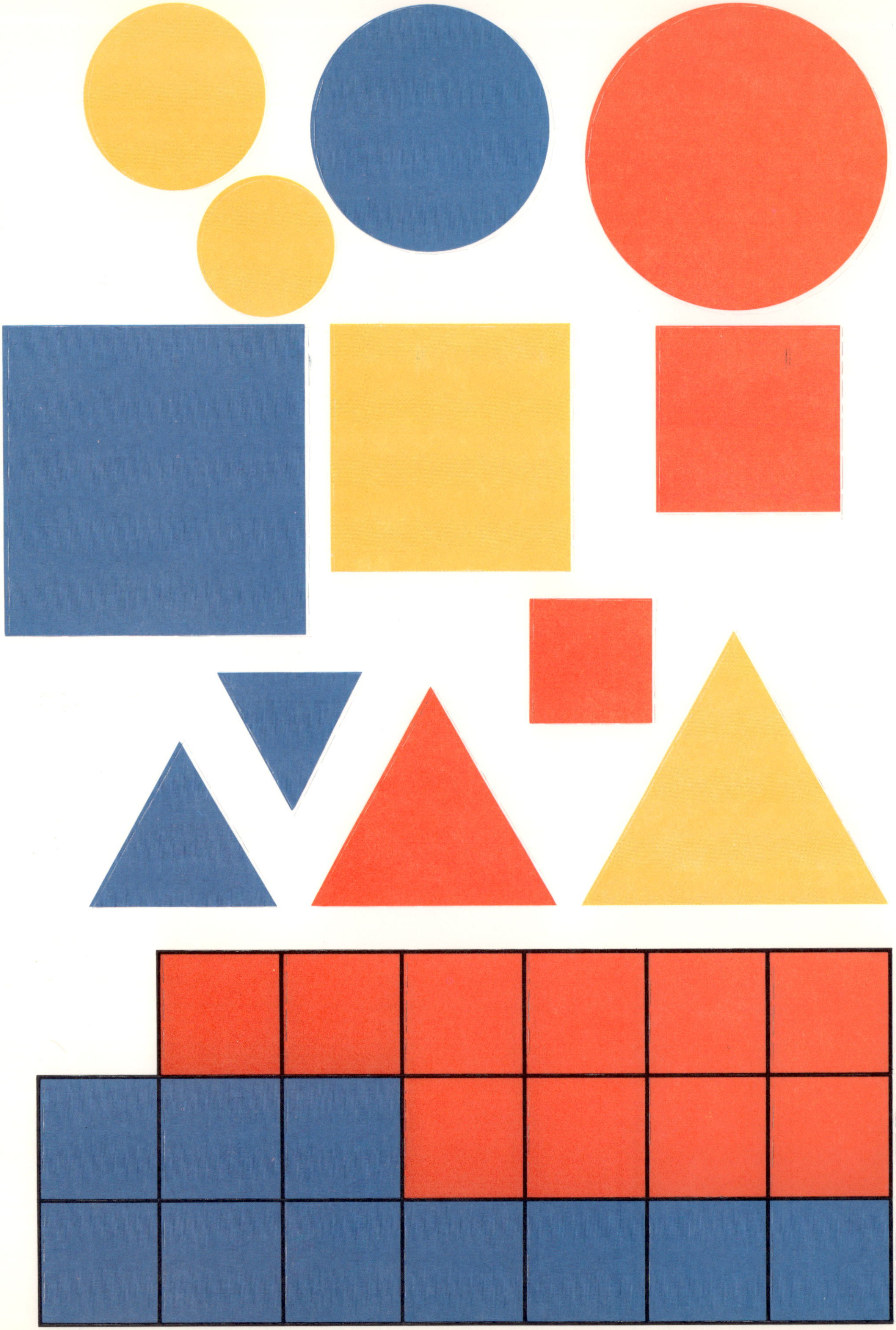

0 1 2 3 4 5 6 7 8 9 10 11 12

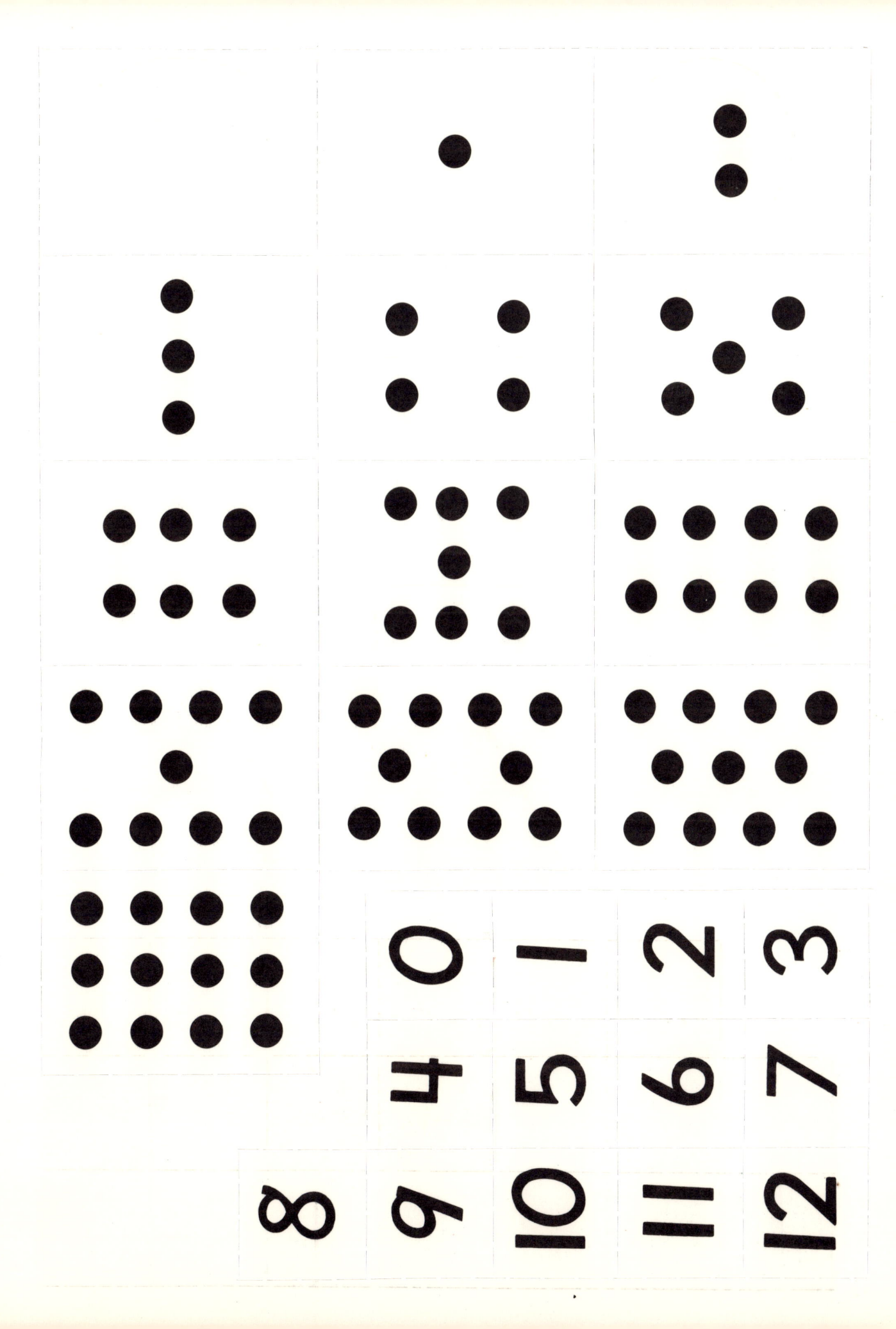

0	3	6	9	12
1	4	7	10	
2	5	8	11	

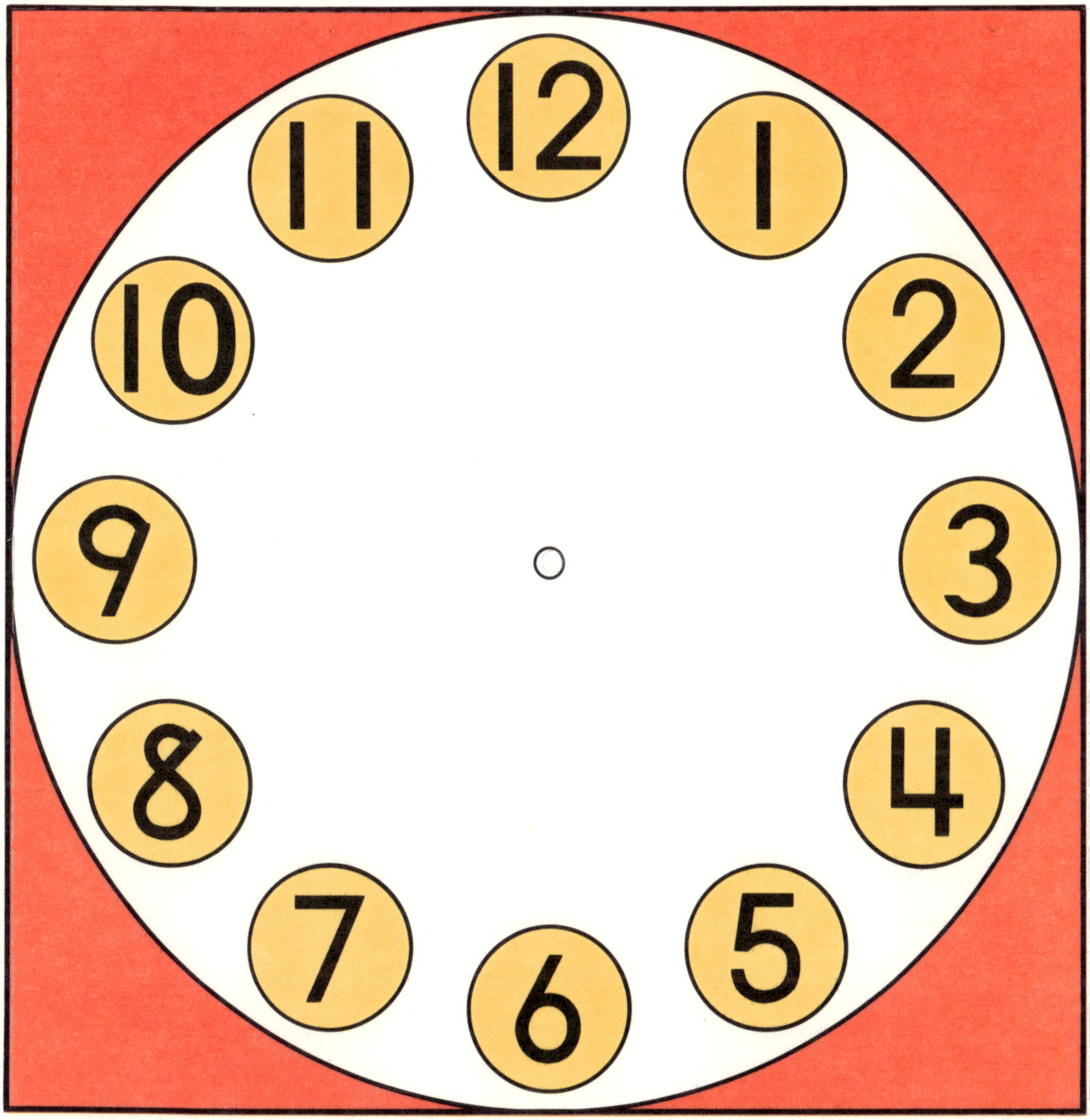
12
1
2
3
4
5
6
7
8
9
10
11

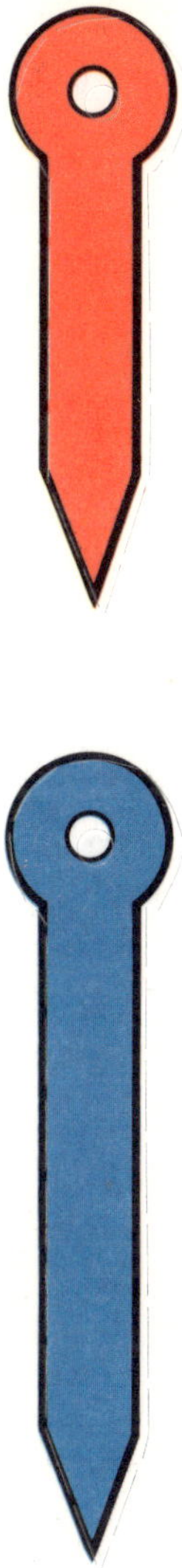

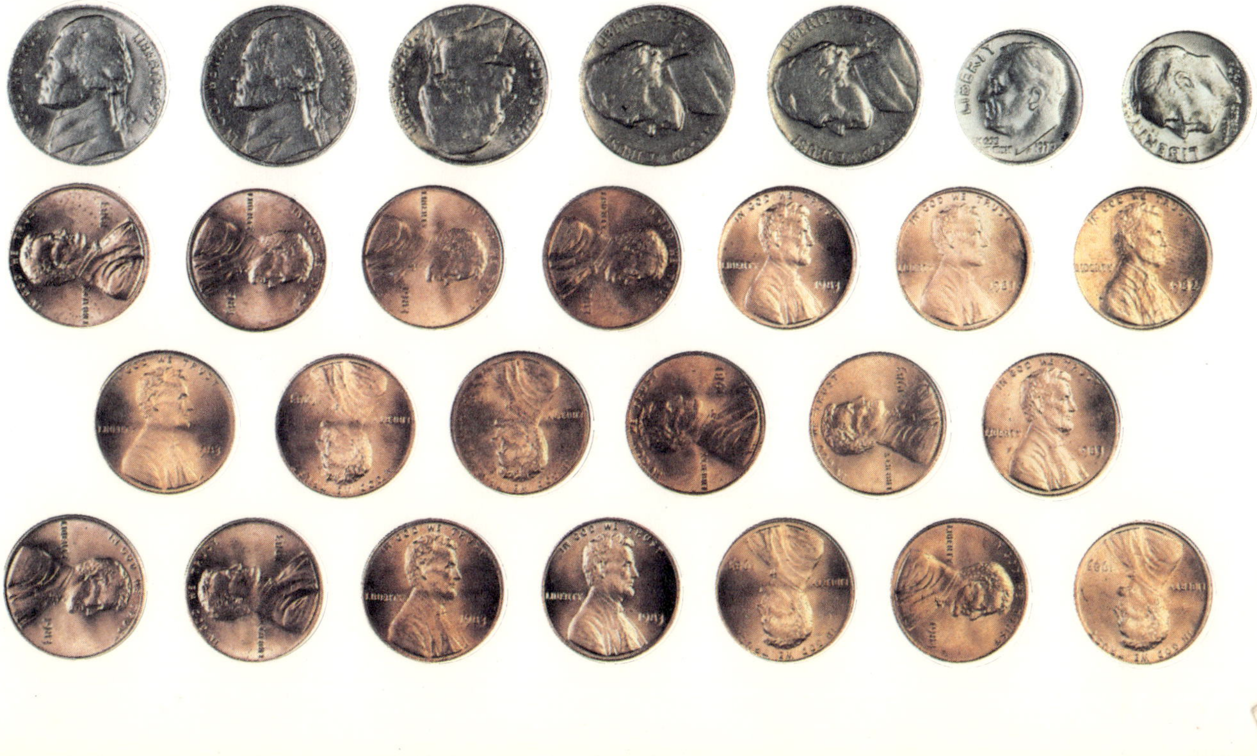

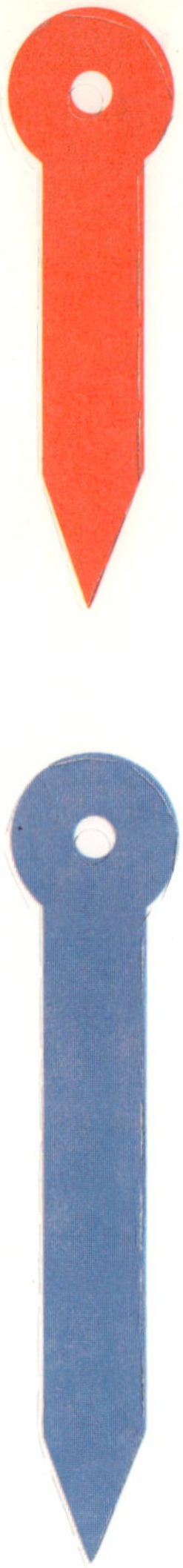

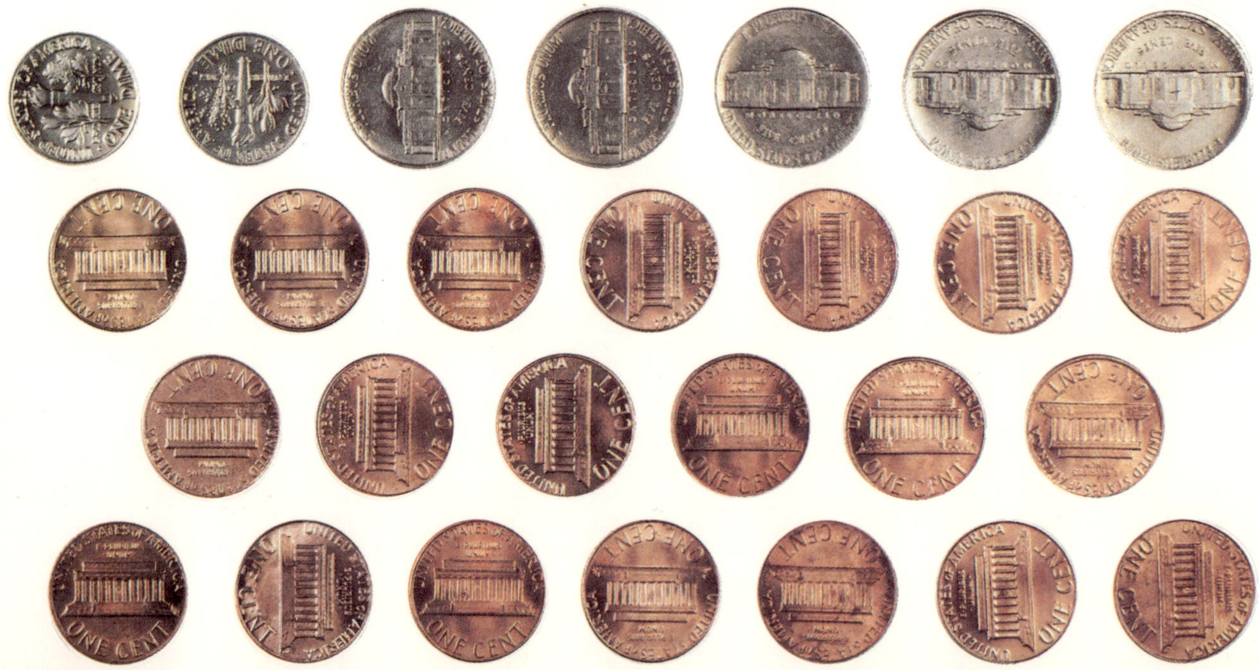

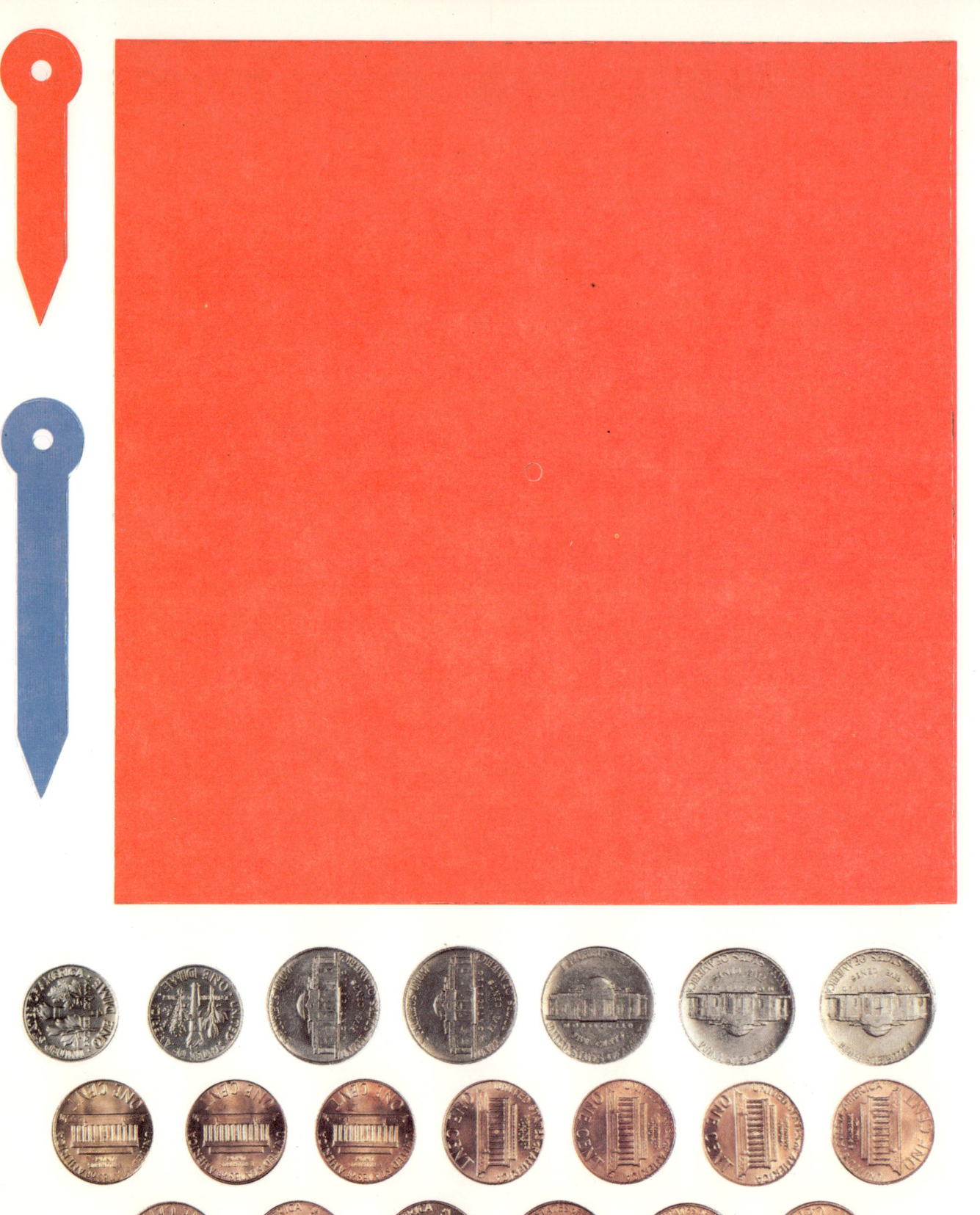